Second Grade

Workbook

Table of Contents

Second Grade

A NOTE TO PARENTS, CAREGIVERS, AND TEACHERS

The *Ready to Learn* series is an excellent tool for assisting your child, grandchild, or student in developing readiness skills in mathematics, reading, and writing during their early learning years. The colorful and engaging workbooks, workpads, and flash cards support the acquisition of foundational skills that all children need to be successful in school and everyday life.

The *Ready to Learn* series develops skills targeted to the Common Core State Standards. The practice workbooks include explanations, strategies, and practice opportunities that engage your young learner with the building blocks needed to become a confident mathematician, reader, and writer. The workpads provide additional practice for the key concepts addressed in the workbooks, and the flash cards support fluency in basic math and reading concepts.

Ready to Learn workbooks include an overview page for each focus area and a certificate at the end of each section to present to your child or student upon completion. It is recommended that you display each certificate earned in a prominent location where your child or student can proudly share that he or she is excited to be a learner!

While the *Ready to Learn* series is designed to support your child's or student's acquisition of foundational skills, it is important that you practice these skills beyond the series. You can do this by having your child or student find examples of what he or she has learned in various environments, such as letters and words on menus at a restaurant, numbers at a grocery store, and colors and shapes on the playground.

Thank you for caring about your child's or student's education. Happy learning!

Reading

Table of Contents

Second Grade Reading Readiness

Second grade is when children become stronger readers by using the strategies and foundational knowledge they have already acquired. Building on that knowledge and adding more advanced decoding skills will help them grow as readers. Talking and writing about what they read will enhance their comprehension skills and foster a love of reading.

Phonics

Initial Sounds

Say the names of the pictures and write the missing letters to complete the words below.

__ irl

__ rog

__ utterfly

__ ruck

__ lock

__ itten

__ ion

__ ake

__ pple

What two words above start with the same sound but different letters?

Final Sounds

Say the names of the pictures and write the missing letters to complete the words below.

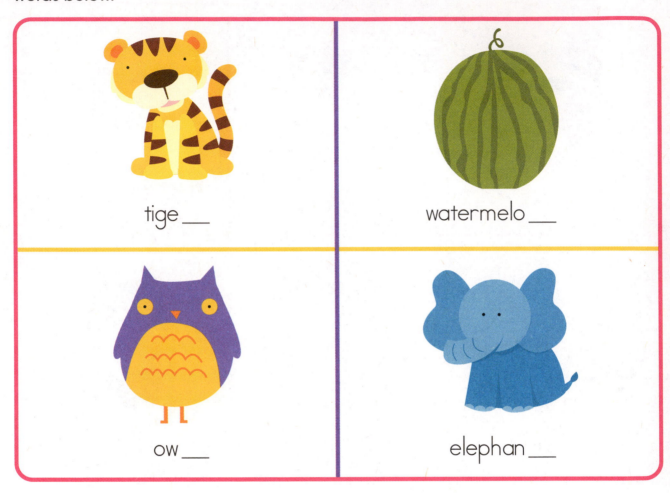

tige ___

watermelo ___

ow ___

elephan ___

Draw something in each box that ends with each letter's sound.

n

m

s

Phonics

Beginning Consonant Blends

br cr fr gr tr

When you see two consonants together, you blend the sounds.
The blended sounds are called consonant blends.

Say the names of the pictures and listen for the consonant blend sounds.
Write the missing letters on the lines below.

__ __ og

__ __ apes

__ __ oom

__ __ umpet

__ __ ab

__ __ een

Phonics

Beginning Consonant Blends

bl cl fl pl

Read the sentences and use the pictures as clues to help you find the missing consonant blends. Write the missing consonant blends on the lines below. Use the list of the beginning consonant blends above to help you.

The butterfly drinks nectar from a _f_ _l_ ower.

I like to __ __ay with my friends.

My brother builds a tower with __ __ocks.

My baby sister likes to carry a __ __anket.

I can tell time on a __ __ock.

I help my mom __ __ean the table.

Earth is the __ __anet we live on.

8

Phonics

Beginning Consonant Blends

st sn sk sp

Say the names of the pictures and listen for the consonant blend sounds.
Write the missing letters on the lines below.

__ __ ake   __ __ airs   __ __ unk

__ __ ider   __ __ oon   __ __ ip

__ __ ates   __ __ owman   __ __ ar

Phonics

Ending Consonant Blends

nt nk mp nd nt

Sometimes consonant blends are at the end of a word. Say the names of the pictures and listen for the consonant blends. Write the missing letters on the lines below.

te__ __

pi__ __

pai__ __

ju __ __

peppermi__ __

sta __ __

la __ __

sa __ __

ha __ __

Phonics

Beginning Consonant Digraphs

th sh ch

A **digraph** is made when **two consonants blend together** and **create one sound**.

Examples: think   ship   chick

Say the names of the pictures and write the missing letters to complete the words below.

__ __eep

__ __urch

__ __eese

__ __ree

__ __umb

__ __oe

__ __air

__ __orn

__ __irt

Phonics

Beginning Consonant Digraphs

kn wr gn

These consonant digraphs are special because you do not hear the first letter, but you *do* hear the second letter's original sound (instead of a new sound).

Examples:

knee   wrap   gnaw

Say the names of the pictures and write the missing letters to complete the words below. Then color the pictures.

_ _ _ ife   _ _ _ ot   _ _ _ eath

_ _ _ ist   _ _ _ at   _ _ _ ome

Ending Consonant Digraphs

ch ck th sh

Sometimes consonant digraphs are at the end of words.

Say the names of the pictures and write the missing letters on the lines below.

chi____   fi____   ba____

di____   sandwi____   bea____

du____   tee____   sti____

Read the text below. Then circle the words with a digraph at the beginning, middle, or end.

My family took a trip to the beach. We brought a picnic with yummy sandwiches. We also packed peaches and juice! We went swimming in the ocean and saw a bunch of fish.

Long Vowels

When you see an e at the end of a word, it is usually silent.

The silent e at the end of a word makes the other vowel in the word sound like its letter name. This creates a long vowel sound.

Examples:  kite cake bike

Draw a line from the picture to its matching silent e word.

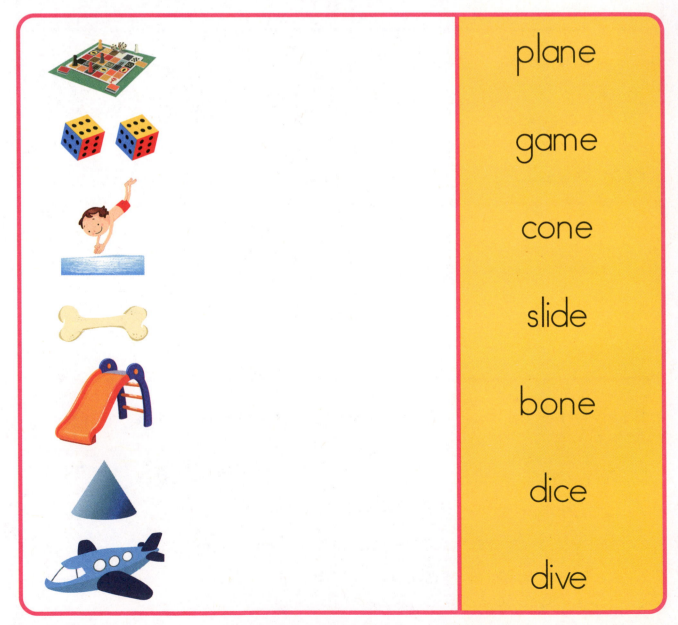

plane

game

cone

slide

bone

dice

dive

Long Vowels

The letter pairs ai and ay both make the long a sound. When a long a word is spelled with ay, the ay is usually at the end of the word. When a long a word is spelled with ai, the ai is usually in the middle of the word.

Look at the pictures below. Circle the correct spelling of the word.

pail   payl   say   sai   tail   tayl

train   trayn   mail   mayl   play   plai

Read the text. Circle the words that have a long a sound.

Hooray! The rain has gone away.

Now it's time to go out and play.

I will see if Gail can come out today.

It is a perfect sailing day!

Long Vowels

The letters ee and ea both make the long e sound.

bee · queen · feet · feed

beans · eat · team · clean

Read the sentences below. Choose the correct ee or ea word from the box above to complete each sentence.

My mom asked me to ___clean___ the table.

My soccer ___team___ won the game.

I love green ___beans___.

My favorite thing to ___eat___ is ice cream.

I ___feed___ my dog every day.

The king is married to the ___queen___.

I am wearing shoes on my ___feet___.

Once, I got stung by a ___bee___.

Long Vowels

The letter **y** at the **end of a word** sometimes makes **the long i sound.** The letters **igh** and **ie** also make the **long i sound.**

Examples:

sky   high   pie

Read the words and write them in the correct **long i** sound category below.

fly   night   spy   tie   light

cry   fries   bright   pie

y	igh	ie
fly		

Phonics

Long Vowels

The letters oa and ow both make the long o sound. Don't be tricked when you read because ow makes another sound too.

Examples:

snow

elbow

boat

Read the words below and draw a picture for each long o sound word.

window

coat

coach

toast

soap

pillow

crow

goat

Long Vowels

The letters **oo** make two unique **long o sounds**, like in b**oo**t and b**oo**k.

Examples: b**oo**t p**oo**l b**oo**k h**oo**k

Draw a line from the picture to its long **oo sound**.

wood

foot

cook

moon

pool

boot

R-controlled Vowels

The letters **er** make the **r sound**. It often comes at the end of a word, but can also be in the middle of a word.

Examples: hamm**er**   p**er**ch

sister   bigger   ladder   teacher

person   mermaid   finger   dinner

Read the sentences below. Choose the correct **er** word from the box above to complete each sentence and write it on the line below.

My brother is _____ than me.

I wish I saw a _____ in the ocean.

I have a bandage on my _____.

I have a little _____.

My _____ reads stories to me.

Our mail carrier is a very nice _____.

My dad climbed a _____ to paint the house.

Every night my family eats _____.

R-controlled Vowels

The letters **ir** also make the **r** sound.

Examples:

chirp

twirl

Draw a line from the picture to the matching **ir** word.

shirt

circus

first

girl

dirt

bird

R-controlled Vowels

The letters **ur** also make the **r sound**.

Examples:

purse

hurt

Read the words below. Draw a picture for each **ur** word.

nurse

burp

surprise

furry

curve

surf

curtain

R-controlled Vowels

The letters **ar** make the sound you hear in st**ar**.
The letters **or** make the sound you hear in st**or**m.

star   storm

arm	car	jar	barn
farm	horn	fork	store

Read the sentences below. Choose the correct **ar** or **or** word from the box above and write it on the line below to complete each sentence.

We took a long drive in the _____.

I broke my _____ and need a cast.

I can't wait to go to the toy _____.

Did you hear the loud _____?

The jam is in a _____.

Pigs live on a _____.

I eat salad with a _____.

The horse is in the _____.

Soft c and Soft g

The letter c makes two sounds.

It makes a /k/ sound, like in cat.

It also makes a /s/ sound, like in face.
This is what is called a soft sound.

The letter g also makes two sounds.

It makes a /g/ sound, like in goat.

It also makes a /j/ sound, like in giraffe.
This is what is called a soft sound.

When these letters are followed by
y, i, or e, they make soft sounds.

cat face

goat giraffe

Look at the pictures below. Circle the words that have a soft c or soft g sound.

city mice giant

circle orange goose gem

cake mug game

Couplet Rhymes

Couplet Poetry

A **couplet poem** is just **two sentences**. The sentences **end in words that rhyme**.

Example: I found a tiny bug.
It was so cute, I gave it a hug.

I enjoy playing in the park.
My dog comes, too, and loves to bark.

Finish the couplet poems below. Write a second sentence that ends with a word that rhymes with the last word in the first sentence.

Once, I found a pretty shell.

I have a very happy dog.

I love to ride my big red bike.

I made a wish upon a star.

Sight Words

Sight Words

There are some words that are hard to sound out because they do not always follow letter-sound rules and do not have picture clues that can help you. Here are some sight words for you to practice reading and writing. Try making up sentences using these words.

Example: Where is the movie playing?

always	don't	or	us
around	fast	pull	use
another	first	read	very
because	five	right	wash
been	found	sing	where
before	gave	sit	which
best	goes	sleep	why
both	green	tell	wish
buy	it's	their	work
call	made	these	would
cold	many	those	write
does	off	upon	your

Sight Word Practice

Look at the beach scene and write about it on the lines below. Use as many sight words as you can from the previous page as you describe what is happening in the scene.

Author's Purpose

Author's Purpose

When an author writes, they do so for one or more reasons: to entertain, to inform, or to persuade.

Writing to Entertain

Writing to entertain means the author wrote the text for the pleasure of reading. Books that are written to entertain are usually fiction.

Circle the books below that were written to entertain.

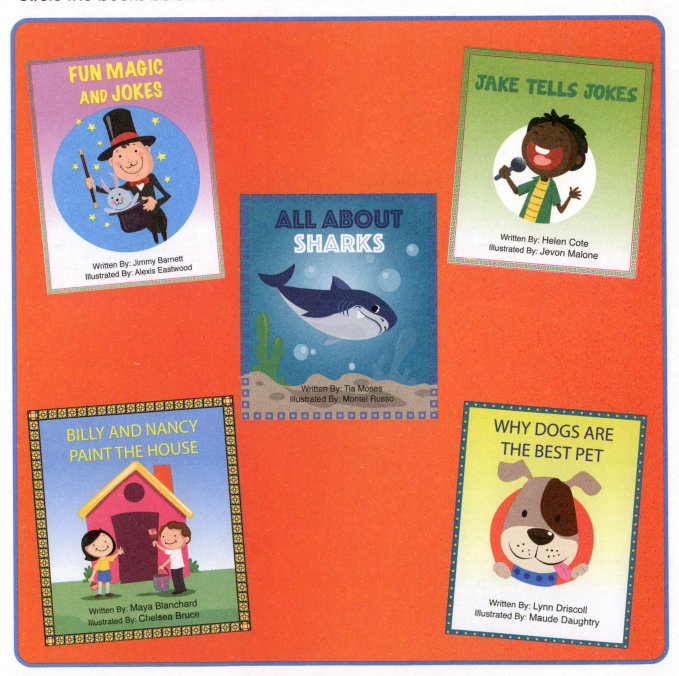

FUN MAGIC AND JOKES
Written By: Jimmy Barnett
Illustrated By: Alexis Eastwood

JAKE TELLS JOKES
Written By: Helen Cote
Illustrated By: Jevon Malone

ALL ABOUT SHARKS
Written By: Tia Moses
Illustrated By: Montel Russo

BILLY AND NANCY PAINT THE HOUSE
Written By: Maya Blanchard
Illustrated By: Chelsea Bruce

WHY DOGS ARE THE BEST PET
Written By: Lynn Driscoll
Illustrated By: Maude Daughtry

Author's Purpose

Writing to Inform

Writing to inform means the author wants to **give readers facts** or **teach them about something**. Books that are written to **inform** are usually **nonfiction**. They can be books **about something or someone**, or they can show readers **how to make or do something**.

Circle the book that was written to **inform**.

Writing to Persuade

Writing to persuade means the author wants to **convince you to believe something** or do something based on **reasons** and **evidence**. Books that are written to **persuade state an opinion** about a topic and then **provide facts** and **explain why** it is important to believe what the author is saying.

Circle the book that was written to **persuade**.

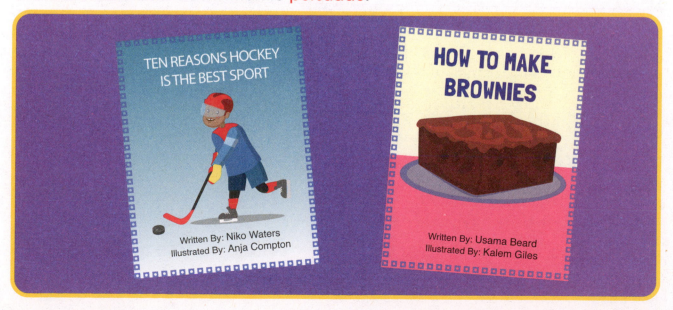

Read the story below.

Hannah's Soccer Game

Hannah was so happy! She had made the starting lineup for her soccer team! It was her third year of playing soccer, and she loved the game. Her favorite position was left fullback. She liked this position because it made her a defender: she had to stop

the other team from getting too close to the goal with the ball. She was really excited about the season and liked her team's chances to win this year.

Halfway through the season, she had played in every game and had stopped the other teams from scoring many times. She felt really comfortable playing the defender position and found it very challenging.

It was now the final game of the season. Hannah's team was playing for the championship. It was near the end of the second half with only five minutes to play. It was tied 2-2. Hannah saw her chance and ran hard with the ball. She eyed the goalie on the other team, and she kicked the ball hard into the corner of the net. GOAL!

It was the last goal of the championship, and her team won it all. Hannah felt like a champion because her team got a trophy! Hannah can't wait for the next soccer season to start again.

Summarizing

Summarizing means explaining the details of the story in just a few words. A story summary should answer these questions: who, what, when, where, and why?

Write a few words or a sentence on each line to answer the questions and summarize "Hannah's Soccer Game."

Who is the main character in the story?

_____

_____

What is happening in the story?

_____

_____

When is it happening?

_____

_____

Where is it happening?

_____

_____

Why did the author write this story? What is the author's purpose?

_____

_____

_____

Main Idea and Important Events

The main idea is what the text is about.

Complete the graphic organizer by writing the main idea and three important events about "Hannah's Soccer Game" in the boxes below.

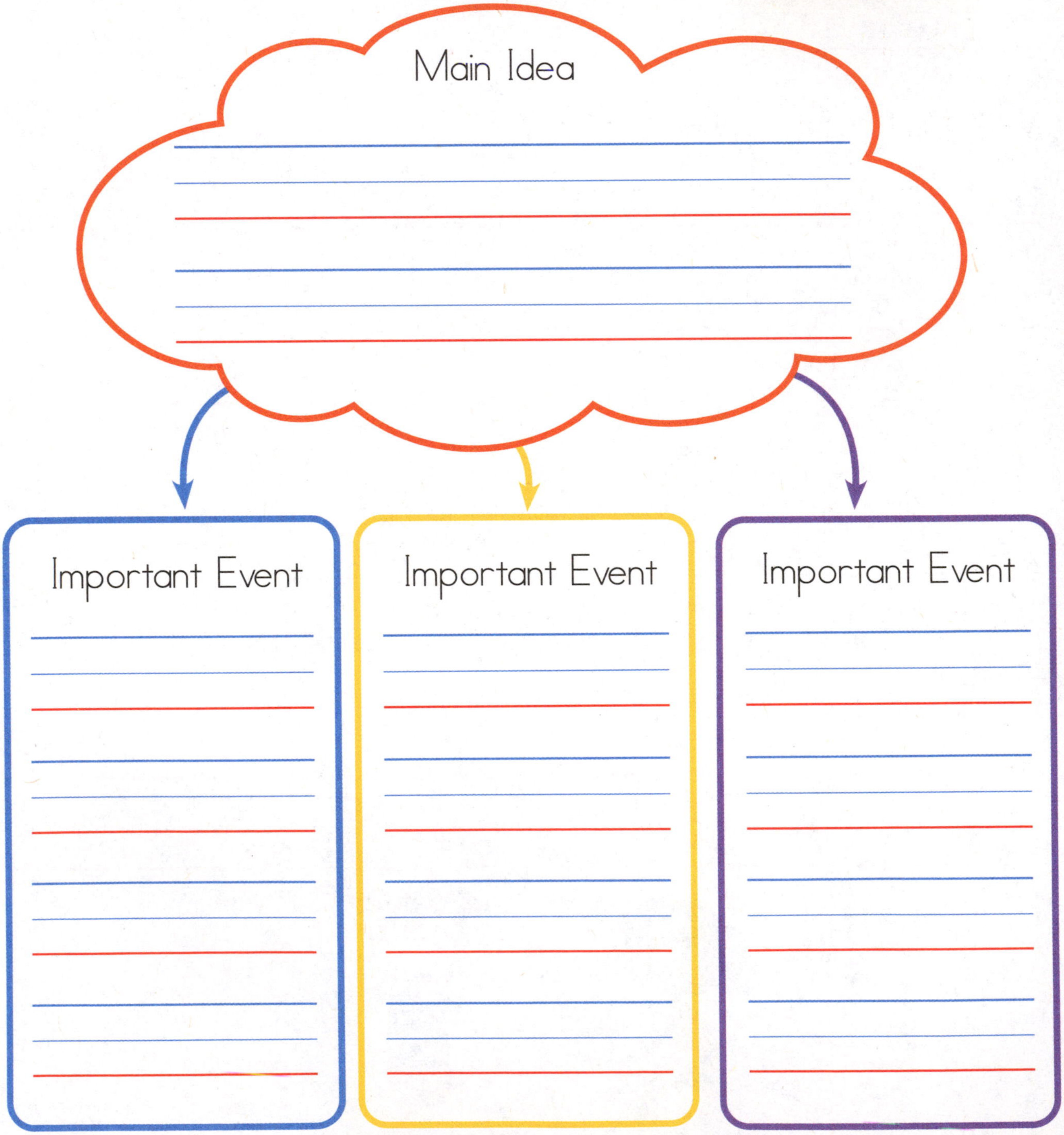

Main Idea

Important Event

Important Event

Important Event

Making Connections

When something in a text reminds readers of something that happened to them, they are making a text-to-self connection!

What connections did you make while reading "Hannah's Soccer Game"?
Write your answers on the lines below.

Think of a time when you felt excited about something.
What were you excited about?

_____
_____
_____
_____

Think of a time when something was a challenge for you.
What was the challenge?

_____
_____
_____
_____

Using the Cover to Predict

The cover of a book can help you predict what is inside.

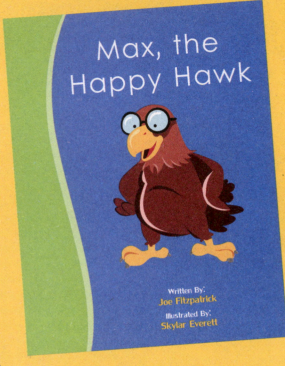

Questions a Book Cover Can Answer:

Max, the Happy Hawk

Written By:
Joe Fitzpatrick

Illustrated By:
Skylar Everett

What is the title? Does it give you a clue about what will be inside?

What is the picture on the cover? Does it give you a clue about what will be inside?

Use the cover above to help you answer these questions. Write your answers on the lines below.

What do you predict this book will be about?

_____

_____

_____

What clue or clues on the cover did you use to make your prediction?

_____

_____

_____

Vocabulary

Unknown Words

If there is a word you do not know in a sentence, studying the words around the unknown word and the illustration can help you figure out what the unknown word means.

Read the sentences below and use the words in each sentence to figure out the missing word.

swooping   **dizzy**   **heights**

Max doesn't like flying too high up in the sky because he is afraid of_____.

After Max spun around too quickly, he got _____ and forgot where he was.

Jax is _____ down quickly to get some food.

Read the story below.

Max, the Happy Hawk

Max loved being a hawk! He loved to hunt for food, and he loved to spend time with his friends, Jax and Pax. His life was great, except for one BIG problem: Max was scared of heights!

He loved to fly because he could get from treetop to treetop quickly. He loved to hunt for mice and fish. He even loved to perch up high on a tree limb and look in every direction, except down! He did not like to look down when he was up high. It scared the feathers right off him!

Hawks tend to hunt for their prey from way up high. They fly in large circles, coasting on updrafts of warm air. Max loved doing this. He loved to fly and feel the sun on his back. He could see far into the distance, even if it was a little cloudy. The problem was that when he got hungry he had to look down. His eyes could pick out the furry blur of a tiny mouse down on the ground far below, but when he looked down, he got dizzy and couldn't swoop down to get his dinner. Max's friend, Pax, suggested he talk to Wise Owl.

Max found Wise Owl and swooped down to perch near him.

"Who, who, whoooo are you?" asked Wise Owl.

"I am Max. I do not like heights, and I get dizzy when I look down!" said Max.

"I think you may need glasses, Max," said Wise Owl.

Wise Owl gave Max a new pair of glasses, and they worked! Max could look down from way up high without getting dizzy. Max REALLY loved flying after that! He didn't get dizzy looking down anymore, and he stopped being afraid of heights. Max was so happy! He was the happiest hawk in the forest!

Visualize What You Read

Draw a picture of the setting for the story "Max, the Happy Hawk." Next, draw each character in the story and be sure to include each character's name.

Main Idea and Important Details

Complete the graphic organizer below by writing the main idea and three important events about "Max, the Happy Hawk" in the boxes below.

Main Idea

Important Event

Important Event

Important Event

Retelling the Story

When you **retell** a story, you tell what happened **in order** from the first event to the last event.

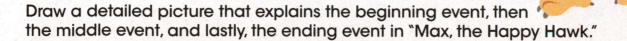

Draw a detailed picture that explains the beginning event, then the middle event, and lastly, the ending event in "Max, the Happy Hawk."

BEGINNING

MIDDLE

END

Finding Important Details

Readers can find important details to answer questions about something they have read. Important details can be found in sentences and illustrations.

What sentence in the story "Max, the Happy Hawk" told you that Max did not like to look down? Write that sentence from the story on the lines below.

Who told Max to go see Wise Owl? Write that sentence from the story on the lines below.

Circle the picture that shows how Max felt when he got glasses.

Circle the word that describes how Max felt after he got glasses.

happy   scared   sad

Making Connections

Make a connection to "Max, the Happy Hawk" and answer the questions. Write your answers on the lines below.

Think of a time when you felt scared.

What were you scared of?

What made you feel better?

Fiction and Nonfiction

Fiction and Nonfiction

A fiction story is a story that is not true.

A nonfiction story is a story that is true. It has facts and information.

Read the stories below and decide whether they are fiction or nonfiction stories. Circle your answer below each story.

A Field Full of Carrots

Rita Rabbit loved eating carrots. She loved them so much that she ate them all day long. One day, Rita woke up and there were no carrots in the house. She went outside to her garden, and there were no carrots there either! Rita began to get very hungry. She ran and ran all the way to Farmer Frank's field. She found carrots as far as the eye could see. "Thank goodness!" she said. Farmer Frank let Rita bring home two big baskets of carrots to share with her family.

Fiction   Nonfiction

Dinosaurs

Dinosaurs cannot be found on Earth anymore. They are extinct. That means there are no more living dinosaurs. Scientists have researched dinosaurs by digging up fossils and dinosaur bones. They found that some dinosaurs ate meat and some ate plants. There used to be many different kinds of dinosaurs.

Fiction   Nonfiction

Table of Contents

The table of contents tells readers which topics can be found in a book and the pages where they can be found.

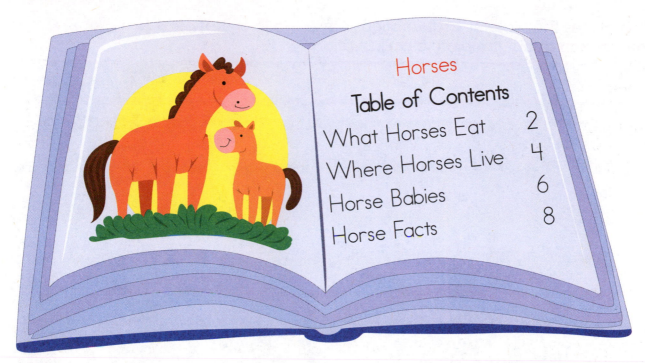

Use the table of contents above to answer the questions. Write your answers on the lines below.

How many topics are in the book?

Which topic begins on page 4?

Which topic begins on page 6?

If I want to find out what horses eat, what topic will help me learn this information?

Nonfiction

Photos and Illustrations

Nonfiction text often has photographs and realistic illustrations. They are meant to give the reader a realistic idea of what things actually look like.

Sometimes the pictures or illustrations have captions that provide more information about the picture or illustration.

Butterflies need to live near a water source, such as a stream or pond.

Use the illustration and caption to answer the questions below.

What do you see in the illustration?

What does the caption tell you about the illustration?

Labels
Labels give more information to the readers.
Nonfiction books use labels to identify details in the pictures.

Use the labeled butterfly diagram to answer the questions. Write your answers on the lines below.

How many legs does a butterfly have?

_____

_____

Are the antenna on the top or bottom of a butterfly's body?

_____

_____

What is the head attached to on a butterfly's body?

_____

_____

Nonfiction

Before You Read

Before you read a nonfiction text, think about the topic.

What do you already know about it?

What do you want to know?

Think about sharks.

What questions do you have about sharks?

Write two questions you have on the lines below before you read the text on the next page.

Question 1

Question 2

46

Read the story below.

Super Shark Facts

Sharks are very interesting and exciting animals. They have been around for millions of years. There were sharks swimming in the ocean long before there were dinosaurs.

There are many different types of sharks. Whale sharks are HUGE! They are the biggest fish in the ocean. They eat tiny crustaceans called krill. Great white sharks are serious eating machines. They eat seals and small whales when they get hungry. They have many rows of teeth and grow new rows of teeth all the time. Great white sharks eat as much as eleven tons of food each year, so they really need all those teeth. Great white sharks are very powerful and can swim almost as fast as cars can go on the highway. One of the reasons great white sharks are such good hunters is their fantastic sense of smell. They can detect blood in the water from nearly three miles away! Sharks are awesome!

After You Read

Think about the new information you learned from reading the nonfiction story.

Write two things that you learned from "Super Shark Facts" on the lines below.

1.

2.

What questions do you still have?

Write one thing you still want to know about sharks on the lines below.

Venn Diagrams

A Venn diagram can be used to compare how two or more things are alike and how they are different.

The overlapping parts of a Venn diagram include information about how things are alike. The parts that don't overlap include information about how things are different.

Think about two different kinds of sharks from "Super Shark Facts" and write how they are alike and different in the Venn diagram below.

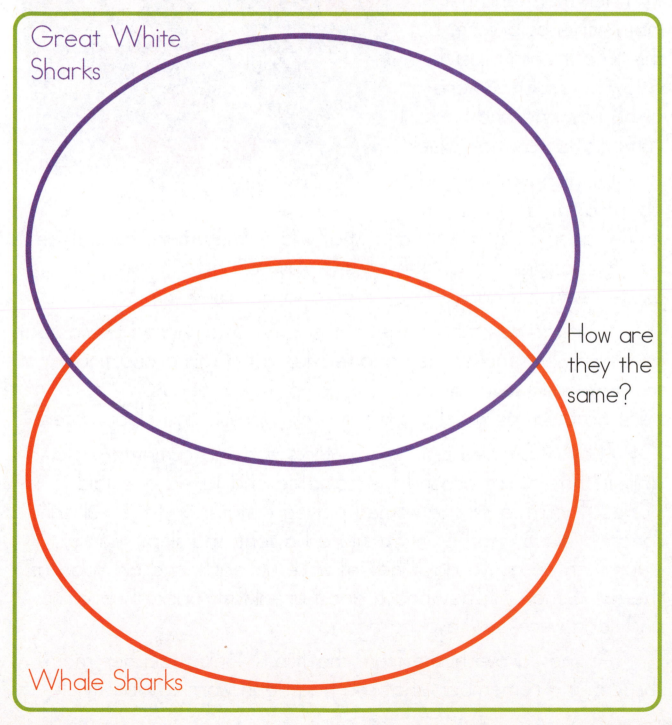

Great White
Sharks

Whale Sharks

How are
they the
same?

Read the story below.

Monica Goes Camping

Monica was worried. She had been kayaking with her mom and her mom's friends before, but this time it wasn't just for a few hours. They were going kayaking and camping for a whole week!

Monica was worried about being so far from home, sleeping in a tent, and what wild animals might be outside her tent at night! Even though she was worried, she was also excited and felt happy to be invited to go along.

Kayaking was fun on the first day. Monica shared a two-seat kayak with her mom. They paddled for a long time and finally got to the place they were going to camp. It was beautiful. There were no buildings in sight, just big rocks, forest, and clear water.

They all pitched in to set up tents and the campsite. After dinner, they all sat around the campfire and talked and told stories. Then two of the women played guitars, and they all sang songs. Monica and her mom shared a tent and slept soundly after such an active day. They all woke up early and did yoga as the sun came up. They had a good breakfast, packed up camp, and soon were out kayaking again.

As they drove home from the trip, Monica told her mom she couldn't remember what she had been worried about!

Visualization

Draw a picture of your favorite part of "Monica Goes Camping."

Keep Reading!

Remember, good readers read every day! Choose any book you like, find a comfortable place, and start reading.

Fill out the reading log below for every book you read.

Independent Reading Log

Book Title	Did you enjoy the book?	Fiction or Nonfiction? Explain how you know.
	👍 👎	
	👍 👎	
	👍 👎	
	👍 👎	

Keep Reading!

Fill out the reading log below for every book you read.

Independent Reading Log

Book Title	Did you enjoy the book?	Fiction or Nonfiction? Explain how you know.
	👍 👎	
	👍 👎	
	👍 👎	
	👍 👎	

CERTIFICATE
of Achievement

....

has sucessfully completed
2nd Grade Reading

Signed: ....

Date: ....

Writing

Table of Contents

Second Grade Writing Readiness

Children in second grade typically enjoy being imaginative and informational writers. They expand their understanding of how to brainstorm so they can write for different purposes. Encourage your child by providing them with opportunities to write. Write notes to each other on whiteboards or set up a writing corner and watch your child become an author!

Aa, Bb, and Cc

Practice writing the uppercase and lowercase cursive letters on the lines below.

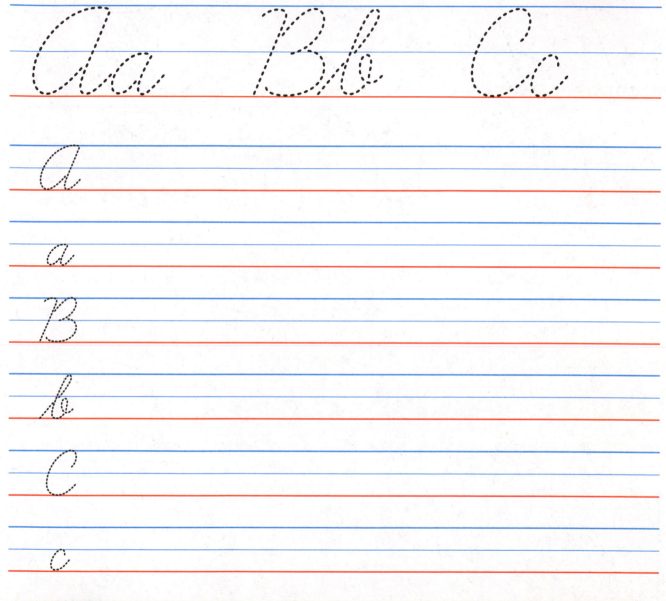

Aa   *Bb*   *Cc*

a

a

B

b

C

c

Dd, Ee, and Ff

Practice writing the uppercase and lowercase cursive letters on the lines below.

Dd   *Ee*   *Ff*

D

d

E

e

F

f

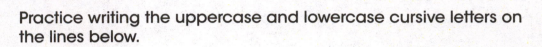

Gg, Hh, and Ii

Practice writing the uppercase and lowercase cursive letters on the lines below.

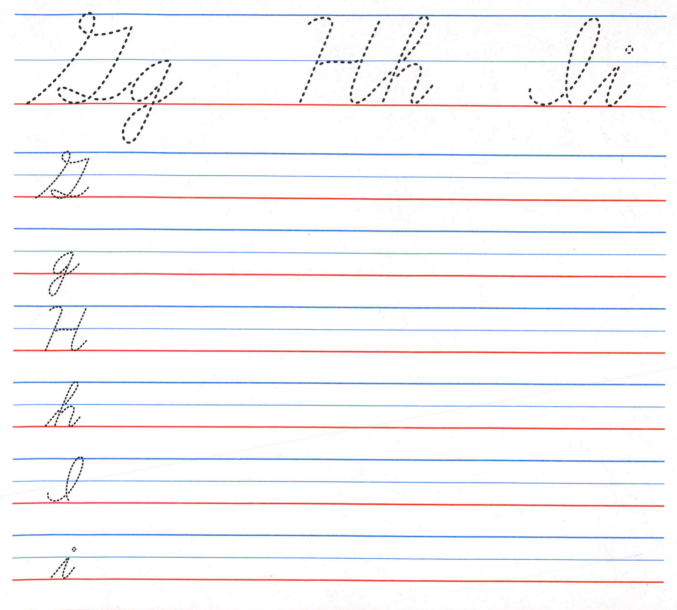

Jj, Kk, and Ll

Practice writing the uppercase and lowercase cursive letters on the lines below.

Mm, Nn, and Oo

Practice writing the uppercase and lowercase cursive letters on the lines below.

Mm Nn Oo

M

m

N

n

O

o

Pp, Qq, and Rr

Practice writing the uppercase and lowercase cursive letters on the lines below.

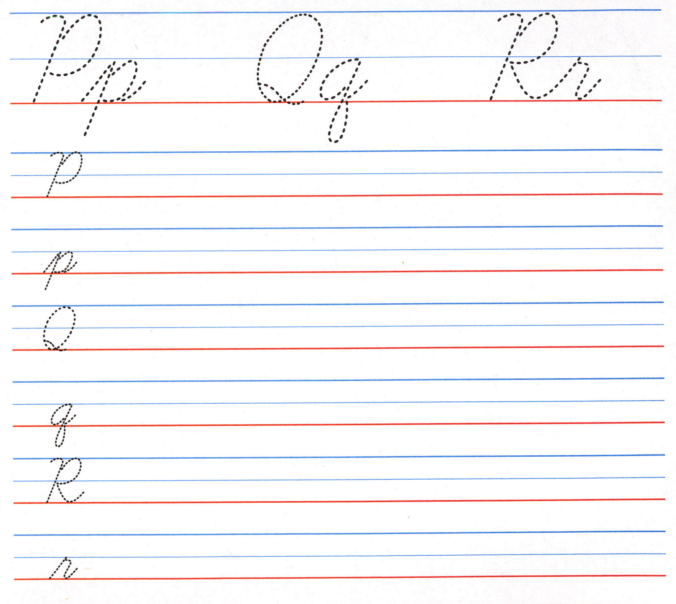

Pp   Qq   Rr

P

p

Q

q

R

r

Ss, Tt, and Uu

Practice writing the uppercase and lowercase cursive letters on the lines below.

Ss Tt Uu

S

s

T

t

U

u

63

Vv, Ww, and Xx

Practice writing the uppercase and lowercase cursive letters on the lines below.

Vv   Ww   Xx

V

Xx

v

W

w

X

x

Yy and Zz

Practice writing the uppercase and lowercase cursive letters on the lines below.

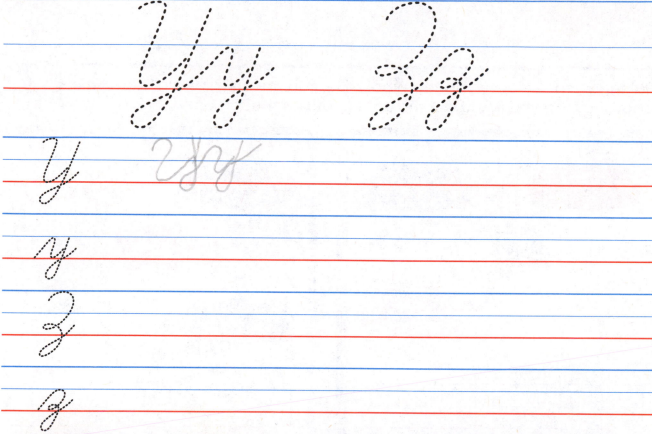

ABC Order

Putting words into **ABC order** means they are **in the order of the alphabet**. Sometimes you need to look at the second or third letter to decide the correct order.

A B C D E F G H I J K L M
N O P Q R S T U V W X Y Z

Put the words below in alphabetical order. You can use the alphabet letters above to help you figure out the correct order for each box.

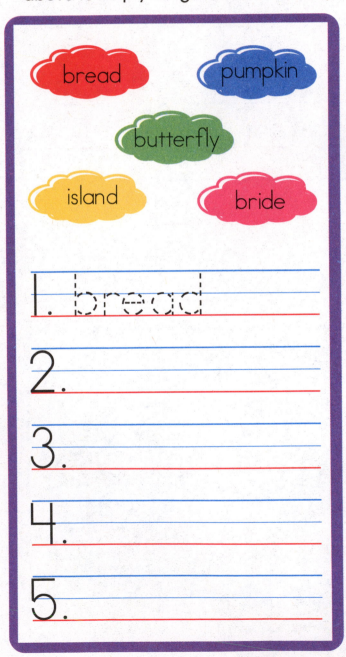

bread   pumpkin   butterfly   island   bride

1. bread
2.
3.
4.
5.

zebra   car   candy   music   cello

1.
2.
3.
4.
5.

Consonants and Vowels

Consonants and Vowels

Some of the letters of the alphabet are vowels, including a, e, i, o, u, and sometimes y. The rest of the letters in the alphabet are called consonants.

Read the words below and circle the vowels in red and circle the consonants in blue.

carrot

lion

pumpkin

flower

turtle

horse

sea star

shoes

duck

lollipop

frog

octopus

Consonants and Vowels

Short and Long Vowels

Vowels most commonly make short vowel sounds, as in dad, jet, gift, fog, and bug.

Vowels can also make long vowel sounds, as in gate, bean, bike, blow, and music.

Look at the pictures and write the missing short or long vowels on the lines below. Say the sounds as you write the letters.

Gwd job! 20/20

c A t   m U sic

p i g   pl A ne

d o g   p i e

b A ll   sn A ke

d U ck   c U be

t o p   b o wl

h A t   h A y

p o t   b i ke

f A n   wh A le

b A t   n i ght

Consonants and Vowels

Short and Long Vowels

Read the words in the bubbles. Color the short vowel words red and the long vowel words blue.

Word Families

Word Families

Word families are words that all share **the same word chunk or letters**.

Examples: cat, hat, mat, and flat are all part of the **at** word family.

Write beginning sounds to create words in each word family below. Try to fill all the lists.

ock	all	ing	ish
__ock	__all	__ing	__ish
__ock	__all	__ing	__ish
__ock	__all	__ing	__ish
__ock	__all	__ing	____ish
____ock	____all	____ing	____ish
____ock	____all	____ing	____ish

70

Word Families

Word Families

Write beginning sounds to create words in each word family. Try to fill all the lists.

   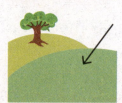

ick	ell	ack	ill
__ick	__ell	__ack	__ill
__ick	__ell	__ack	__ill
__ick	__ell	__ack	__ill
__ick	__ell	__ack	__ill
__ __ick	__ __ell	__ __ack	__ __ill
__ __ick	__ __ell	__ __ack	__ __ill

Prefixes

Prefixes

A **prefix** attaches to the **beginning** of a **root word** to create a **new word** with a **different meaning**.

Prefix meanings: **un**: not, or the opposite of
                   re: again
                   pre: before

Example: **un**happy **means** **not** happy

Read the words below. Add the prefix to make a new word with a new meaning.

Add **un**.

____tied   ____happy   ____locked

Add **re**.

____turn   ____do   ____play

Add **pre**.

____school   ____heat   ____view

72

Suffixes

Suffixes

A **suffix** attaches to the **end** of a root word to create a **new word** with a **different meaning**.

Suffix meanings: **er**: more
est: most

Example: bigg**er** means it is larger than big, and bigg**est** means it is the largest.

Read the words below.

| tall | dark | light | short | fast |

Add the suffixes to make new words with new meanings. Write each word with the first suffix in the first column. Write each word with the second suffix in the second column.

er	est
taller	tallest

Synonyms

Synonyms

Synonyms are different words that have the **same, or almost the same, meaning.**

Example: happy and glad

Draw a line to match each word in the first column to its synonym.

fast	begin
wet	afraid
pretty	quick
smart	simple
little	tidy
scared	beautiful
start	too
also	small
clean	damp
easy	clever

Antonyms

Antonyms are words that mean **the opposite**.

Example: happy and sad

Draw a line to match each word in the first column to its antonym.

hot	down
front	night
day	cold
clean	dirty
up	back

Draw two pictures that illustrate two **antonym** words. Write your antonym word under each picture.

Plural Nouns

Plural means **more than one**.

To make most nouns plural, you add an **s**. If the noun ends in **ch**, **sh**, **s**, **x**, or **z**, you add **es**.

Example:

one frog   →   two frog**s**   one fox   →   two fox**es**

Read the words below.

dress	kiss	dish	cat	park
book	girl	room	lunch	glass

Write the words with s or es on the lines below in the correct column.

s	es

Present and Past Tense

Present Tense and Past Tense

Present tense means an action that is happening right now. To make a word present tense, you add ing to the end of the word.

Example: play becomes playing

Past tense means an action that has already happened. To make a word past tense, you add ed to the end of the word.

Example: play becomes played

Roll a die. Write the word that matches the number you rolled in the past and present tense. Roll until you get each word.

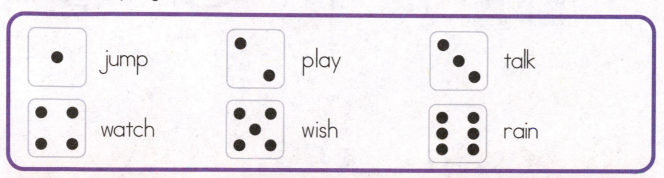

jump play talk

watch wish rain

PAST	PRESENT

Common Nouns

Common Nouns

Common nouns are words for people, animals, places, and things.

horse

boy

bike

books

shoes

giraffe

Use the nouns from the pictures above to fill in the missing words in the sentences.

A _____ has a very long neck.

The _____ is wearing a blue shirt.

I ride my _____ to school every day.

I fed a _____ at the farm.

I learned how to tie my _____ today.

She likes to read her _____.

Common Nouns

Common Nouns

Circle the common nouns in the nursery rhyme lines below.

Twinkle, twinkle, little star.

He sat on a wall.

They went up the hill.

She had a little lamb.

The dish ran away with the spoon.

Baa, baa, black sheep.

Common and Proper Nouns

A proper noun is a noun that is the name of something. Proper nouns always have a capital letter at the beginning of the word.

Examples: teacher is a common noun.

Mrs. Everett is a proper noun because it is the teacher's name.

Color the proper nouns purple. Color the common nouns yellow.

80

Common and Proper Nouns

Common and Proper Nouns

Identify the pictures as common or proper nouns. Then write the word common or proper next to each picture.

bear _____

squirrel _____

tent _____

hat _____

Mr. Hunter _____

Seattle _____

United States _____

octopus _____

Zac _____

Hannah _____

tiger _____

moose _____

Kristin _____

castle _____

koala _____

April _____

Adjectives

Adjectives are words that describe how things feel, smell, taste, or sound.

Read the words in each row. Circle the two words that describe each picture.

pink	hot	slippery	dirty
fluffy	gray	black	smelly
cold	bright	purple	hot

Add an adjective that describes the noun in each sentence.

Kittens are _____ .

Candy is _____ .

Rain is _____ .

Fire is _____ .

Friends are _____ .

Dogs are _____ .

Alligators are _____ .

Adjectives

Adjectives

Draw an imaginary monster friend in the box below. Be sure to include a lot of details!

Answer questions about your monster friend on the lines below.

How would you describe your monster friend?

What color or colors describe your monster friend?

How is your monster friend feeling?

What are some other words that describe your monster friend?

Verbs

Verbs

Verbs are words that **tell what a noun is doing.** They are **action words.**

Use the picture above to help you complete the sentences. Write the words on the lines below.

The friends are _____ snowballs.

The kids are _____ in the snow.

The girl is _____ on the swing.

The moms are _____ to each other.

The dad is _____ coffee.

The boy and girl are _____ a snowman.

The people are _____ on the ice.

Verbs

Verbs

Read the words below.

Color the winter hats that have verbs on them.

skip   bird   hand   wiggle   nose

cup   talk   game   run   laugh

Read the sentences below. Then circle the correct verb to complete each sentence.

I love to (jumping, jump) rope.

I am (play, playing) a game.

The cow is (eat, eating) the grass.

Can we (go, going) to the playground?

I love (drink, drinking) hot chocolate!
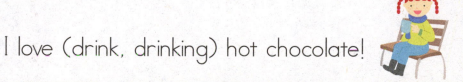

Verbs and Adverbs

Verbs and Adverbs

Adverbs are words that give more information about a verb and can make your writing more interesting.

Example: The girl danced beautifully.

Adverbs can answer the questions below.

How?	How often?	Where?	When?
easily	never	outside	now
happily	often	inside	early
loudly	seldom	here	after
quickly	once	everywhere	before
softly	sometimes	home	soon
slowly	always	away	today
silently	daily	there	since

Using the list above, add an adverb to each sentence to make it more interesting.

I can tie my shoes _____.

Do you play the drums _____?

I can read my book _____.

They play soccer _____.

I have dance class _____.

Verbs and Adverbs

Verbs and Adverbs

Circle the verb and underline the adverb for each sentence below. Then write the verb and adverb for each sentence in the correct columns.

verb	adverb
hopped	quickly

The rabbit (hopped) quickly.

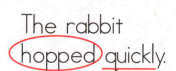

The drummer plays often.

She wraps the gifts carefully.

The ballerina dances gracefully.

We watched a movie outside.

We slept comfortably.

I walked softly.

Compound Words

Compound Words

Compound words are two words put together to make a new word with a new meaning.

Example: paint and brush = paintbrush

Look at the pictures below and say the words. Put the two words together and write the compound word on the lines below.

sun + flower	=	sunflower
horse + shoe	=	
cat + fish	=	
eye + ball	=	
pig + pen	=	
dog + house	=	
cup + cake	=	
lip + stick	=	

Compound Words

Draw a line to match two socks to make a real compound word. Write your compound words on the lines below.

Contractions

Contractions are two words made into one word. An apostrophe is placed where some of the letters are left out of the new word.

Example: do not = don't

Draw a line from the words to the matching contractions.

did not	isn't
was not	didn't
have not	wasn't
is not	haven't

I will	you'll
you will	I'll
they will	she'll
she will	they'll

I am	she's
he is	I'm
she is	he's
it is	it's

Contractions

Contractions

Read the two words in each box and write its contraction on the lines below.
Then color the animals.

did not

was not

have not

is not

I am

he is

she is

it is

I will

you will

they will

she will

Writing Sentences

Sentences

Every sentence starts with a capital letter and ends with a punctuation mark.

Statement sentences tell the reader something. They start with a capital letter and end with a period.

Read the statement sentences. Rewrite them on the lines below using a capital letter at the beginning and ending with a period.

i like to play at the park

_____

let's go swimming today

_____

i live in the United States

_____

the frog jumped over the log

_____

i can feed the chickens on the farm

_____

my name is Emma

_____

i can skate really well

_____

Narrative Writing

Narrative writing is writing a story with a beginning, middle, and end.

Complete the graphic organizer below to help you brainstorm ideas. Think of a time you played with a friend. What happened first? What happened next? What happened then? And what happened last? Draw pictures or write a few idea words in each box to plan your story writing.

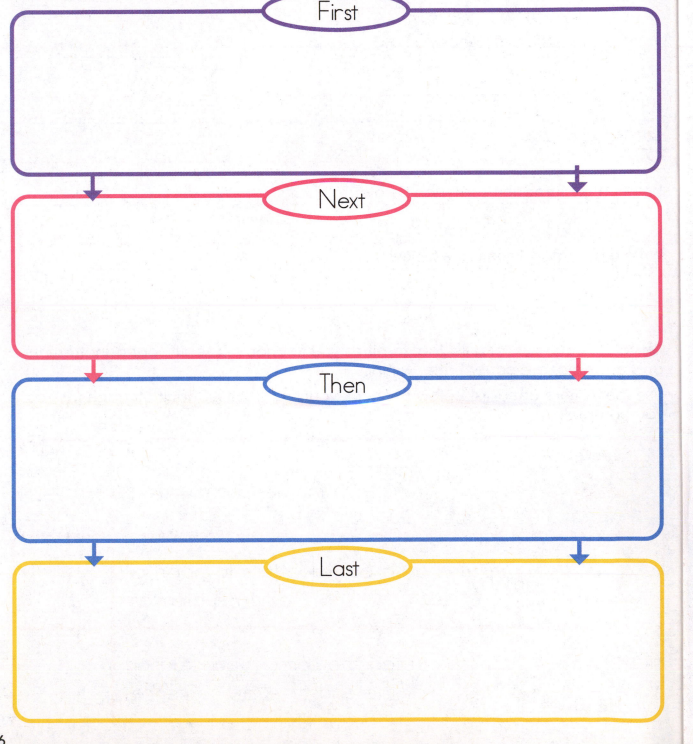

First

Next

Then

Last

Sentences

Question sentences ask the reader a question. They start with a capital letter and end with a question mark.

Read the question sentences. Rewrite them on the lines below using a capital letter at the beginning and ending with a question mark.

what is your favorite sport

do you know how to tie your shoes

can you come out to play today

what is your favorite color

what grade are you in

who is your best friend

where do you live

Sentences

Exclamation sentences tell the reader about something that is exciting, scary, or surprising. They start with a capital letter and end with an exclamation mark.

Commands are short sentences with only a noun and verb. Commands also start with a capital letter and end with an exclamation mark.

Read the sentences. Rewrite them on the lines below using a capital letter at the beginning and ending with an exclamation mark.

look at that scary monster

i won the race

look at the beautiful fireworks

sit down

go, team

it is my birthday today

look out

Sentences

Write two statement sentences below.

Write two question sentences below.

Write an exclamation sentence below.

Write a command sentence below.

An editor's checklist is a list that reminds you to check to see if your punctuation and grammar are correct after writing.

Use the editor's checklist below to check your sentences. Check off each task as you complete it.

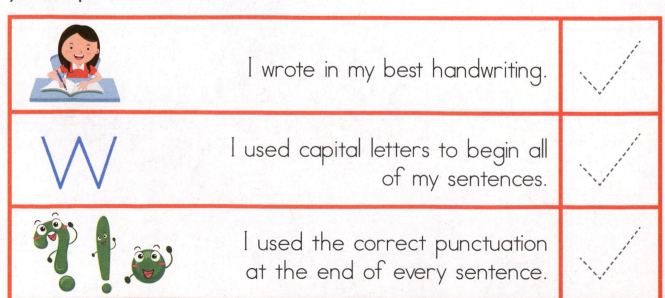

	I wrote in my best handwriting.	✓
W	I used capital letters to begin all of my sentences.	✓
	I used the correct punctuation at the end of every sentence.	✓

Narrative Writing

Narrative Writing

Use the graphic organizer below and write complete sentences to share the details of your brainstormed ideas.

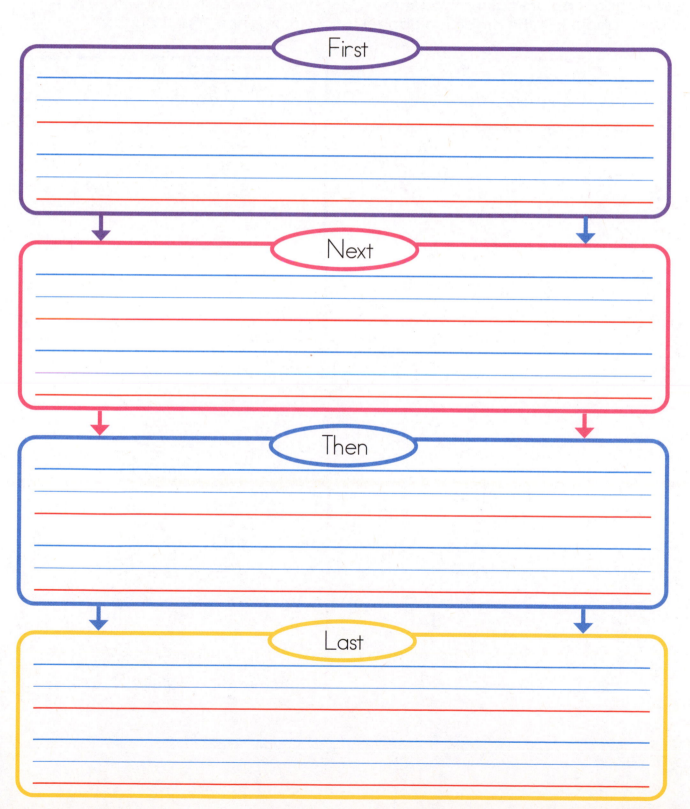

First

Next

Then

Last

Informational Writing

Informational Writing

Informational writing is writing about a topic and providing details to help readers understand more about the topic.

Write about an animal that you know a lot about. Draw pictures or write a few words about it in the graphic organizer below to organize your thoughts.

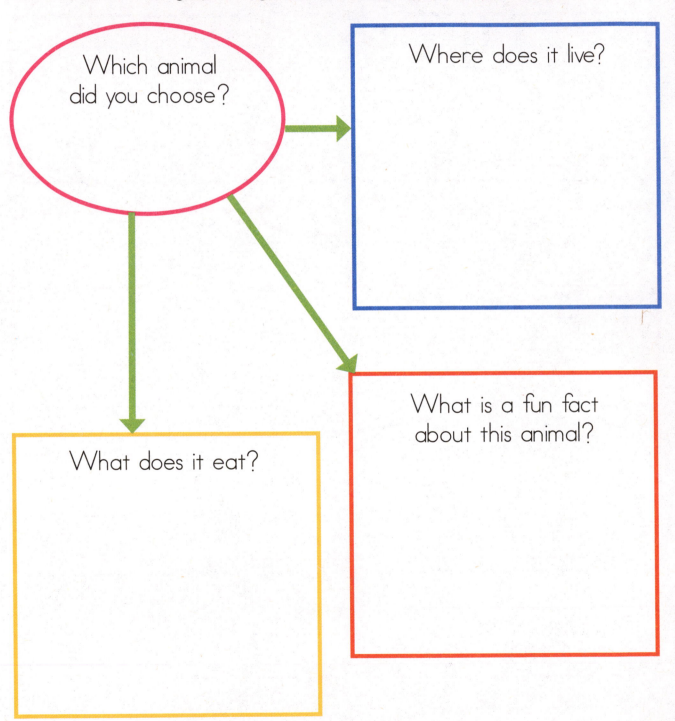

Which animal did you choose?

Where does it live?

What does it eat?

What is a fun fact about this animal?

Informational Writing

Informational Writing

Look at your graphic organizer and write sentences based on your brainstormed ideas.

I know a lot about...

It lives...

It eats...

A fun fact about this animal is...

Opinion Writing

Opinion Writing

Opinion writing is writing about **something you believe** and giving **reasons for why you believe it**.

Write your opinion about your favorite activity to do outside. What are three reasons why you like it? Draw pictures or write a few words to organize your thoughts in the graphic organizer below.

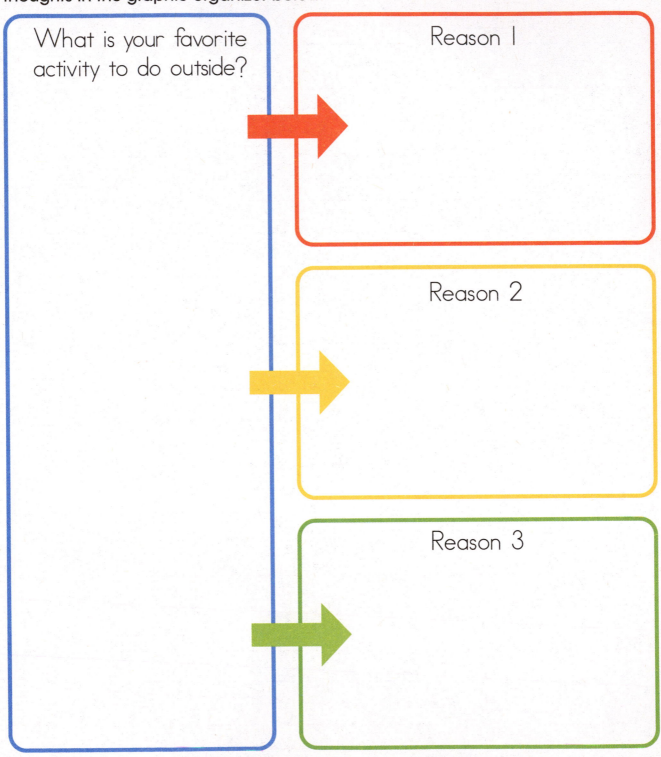

What is your favorite activity to do outside?

Reason 1

Reason 2

Reason 3

Opinion Writing

Opinion Writing

Look at your graphic organizer and write sentences based on your brainstormed ideas.

My favorite activity to do outside is...

I like it because...

I also like it because...

It is really fun because...

Explanation Writing

Explanation writing is writing to **teach the reader how to do something.** You write the steps and draw pictures to illustrate what the steps look like.

In the boxes below, draw pictures and write a few words that explain how to build a snowman.

How to Build a Snowman

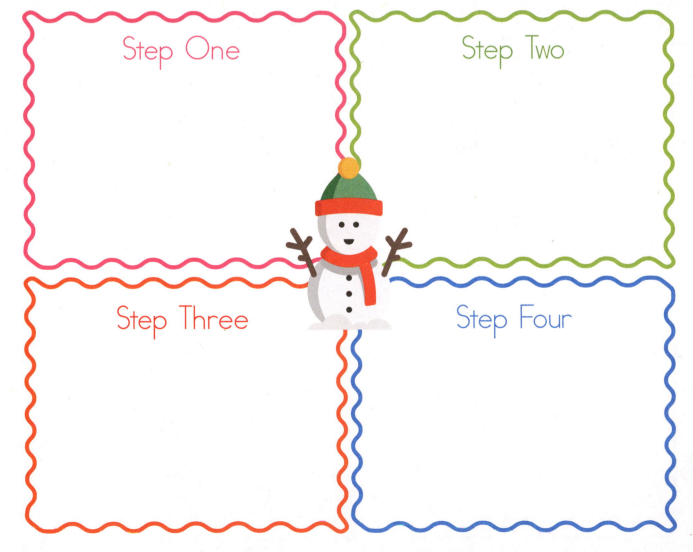

Step One

Step Two

Step Three

Step Four

Explanation Writing

Use the graphic organizer to write complete sentences to explain each step to a reader.

How to Build a Snowman

Step One

_____

_____

Step Two

_____

_____

Step Three

_____

_____

Step Four

_____

_____

Now draw a picture for each step in the boxes below.

1	2
3	4

CERTIFICATE
of Achievement

has successfully completed

2nd Grade Writing

Signed:

Date:

1²3 Math

Table of Contents

Second Grade Math Readiness

By second grade, children are applying the mathematics skills they learned in previous grades to larger numbers and more complex processes. They have a better spatial sense, which allows for a broader range of mathematical ideas to become more accessible. This year, a major developmental shift occurs when second graders begin learning basic multiplication concepts. Strategic thinking games, such as checkers, chess, dominoes, and cribbage, are great for helping build math skills at this age.

Number Patterns

Count by Twos

Skip counting can make counting faster!

Skip count the flowers by 2s per flowerpot. Write the increasing numbers on the lines below as you count.

Number Patterns

Count by Fives

Skip counting by 5s is even faster!

You can count the arms of sea stars quickly because each sea star has five.
Write the increasing number of arms on each one as you count each sea star by 5s.

Number Patterns

Count by Tens

Skip counting by 10s is even faster!

Skip count the jelly beans in each jar by 10s. Write the increasing numbers on the lines below as you count.

Place Value

Hundreds, Tens, and Ones

Look at the illustrations and write the hundreds, tens, and ones on the lines below.

Example:

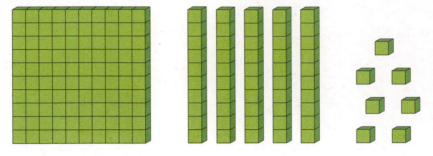

1 hundred **and** 5 tens **and** 7 ones **=** 157

2 hundreds 2 tens 6 ones = 226

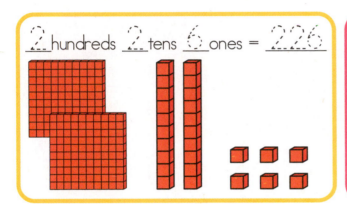

___hundreds ___tens ___ones = _____

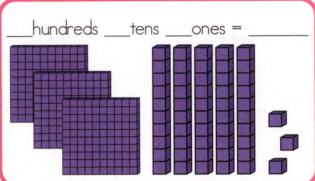

___hundred ___tens ___one = _____

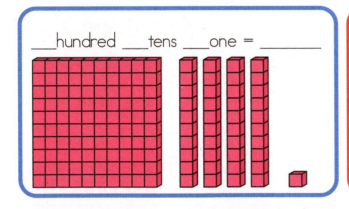

___hundreds ___ten ___ones = _____

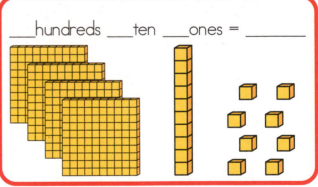

___hundred ___tens ___ones = _____

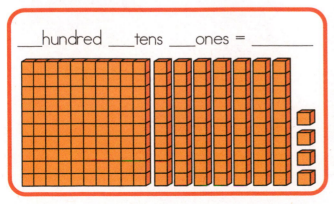

___hundreds ___tens ___ones = _____

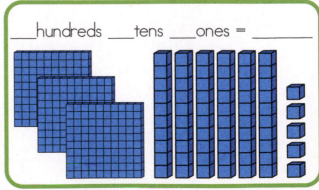

Place Value

Real Situations

Read the math stories and answer the questions.

Libby, a librarian, loves her library books. She has shelves of 100 library books, boxes of 10 books, and single books.

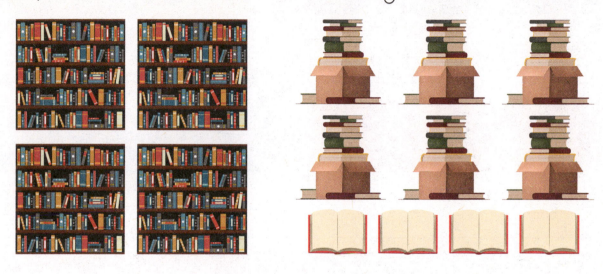

How many books does Libby have? _____

Ben, a zookeeper, needs to feed the seals! He has crates of 100 fish, buckets of 10 fish, and some single fish.

How many fish does Ben have to feed the seals? _____

Place Value

Expanded Form

Write the numbers below in expanded form.

Example: 359 = 300 + 50 + 9

671	283
___ + ___ + ___	___ + ___ + ___
105	920
___ + ___ + ___	___ + ___ + ___
762	334
___ + ___ + ___	___ + ___ + ___
547	999
___ + ___ + ___	___ + ___ + ___
418	856
___ + ___ + ___	___ + ___ + ___

Place Value

Comparing Numbers

Use greater than >, less than <, or equal to = to make the equations **true** and write the number below each expanded number.

300 + 20 + 1 300 + 60 + 1

_3 2 1_   _3 6 1_

900 + 50 + 3 900 + 50 + 1

_____   _____

600 + 0 + 0 600 + 10 + 1

_____   _____

200 + 90 + 9 200 + 80 + 9

_____   _____

100 + 10 + 1 100 + 10 + 1

_____   _____

500 + 30 + 7 500 + 40 + 7

_____   _____

Place Value

Ordering Numbers

Put the following numbers in order from greatest to least.

352, 125, 501

501 , 352 , 125

623, 603, 671

_____ , _____ , _____

901, 989, 931

_____ , _____ , _____

232, 721, 43

_____ , _____ , _____

Put the following numbers in order from least to greatest.

438, 223, 639

223 , 438 , 639

222, 202, 220

_____ , _____ , _____

521, 512, 152

_____ , _____ , _____

726, 861, 672

_____ , _____ , _____

Even Numbers

When the digit in the ones place is 0, 2, 4, 6, or 8, the number is an even number. This means the number can be decomposed into two equal groups.

Example:

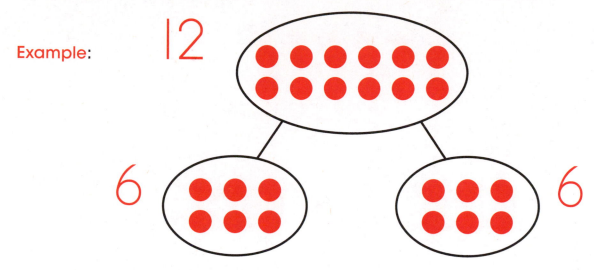

Create equal groups for these numbers. First fill the top oval with the total number of dots. Then divide that number into two equal groups and fill in the bottom two ovals with an equal number of dots.

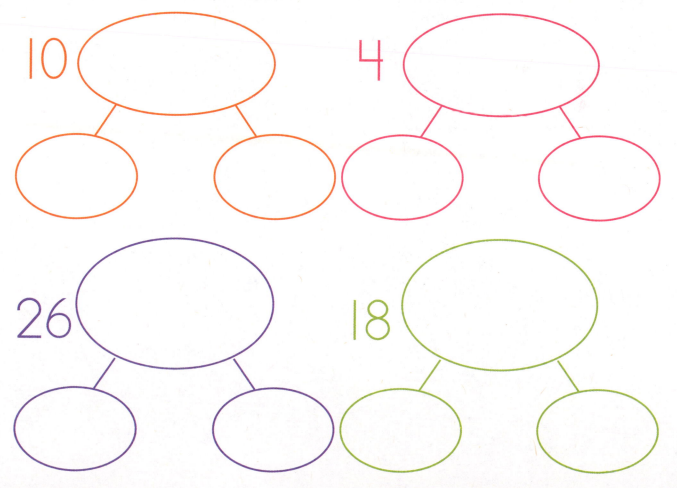

Odd Numbers

When the digit in the ones place is 1, 3, 5, 7, or 9, the number is an odd number. This means the number will have one left over when decomposed into two equal groups.

Example:

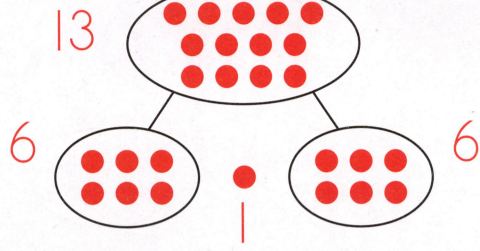

Create equal groups for these numbers. First fill the top oval with the total number of dots. Then divide that number into two equal groups and fill in the bottom two ovals with the correct number of dots. There should be one number left over, so be sure to draw a dot to represent that number between the two ovals.

Operations

Equal/Unequal Equations

Example: even + even = even   12 + 12 = 24
even + odd = odd   12 + 13 = 25
odd + odd = even   13 + 13 = 26

Write double-digit equations below that work for the operation pattern.

even + even = even

26 + 26 = 52

even + odd = odd

____ + ____ = ____

odd + odd = even

____ + ____ = ____

even + even = even

____ + ____ = ____

even + odd = odd

____ + ____ = ____

Operations

Adding 2-Digit Numbers by Traditional Regrouping

Regrouping means **changing ones into tens** or **tens back into ones.**
Adding two-digit numbers often requires regrouping.

Look at the example below. **If the numbers in the ones column add up to more than 9, we need to regroup.**

Example: $45 + 19 =$ ___

First add the ones.

$5 + 9 = 14$.

14 is more than 9. We need to regroup.

14 means 1 ten and 4 ones.

Put the 4 in the ones column
and the 1 at the top of the tens column.

Now add the tens. $10 + 40 + 10 = 60$.

Put your tens and ones together. $60 + 4 = 64$.
The sum is 64.

Tens	Ones
1	
4	5
+ 1	9
6	4

Solve the equations by regrouping. Write the sums in the boxes below.

Tens	Ones
□	
2	6
+ 4	7

Tens	Ones
□	
4	5
+ 3	8

Tens	Ones
□	
2	2
+ 3	9

Tens	Ones
□	
4	7
+ 3	6

Tens	Ones
□	
7	3
+ 1	8

Tens	Ones
□	
4	6
+ 2	8

Tens	Ones
□	
3	6
+ 5	5

Tens	Ones
□	
2	9
+ 6	8

Operations

Adding 2-Digit Numbers by Traditional Regrouping

Solve the equations by regrouping. Write the sums in the boxes below.

Tens	Ones
□	
4	9
+ 1	8

Tens	Ones
□	
2	6
+ 1	7

Tens	Ones
□	
4	7
+ 3	5

Tens	Ones
□	
7	4
+ 1	7

Tens	Ones
□	
1	9
+ 2	7

Tens	Ones
□	
1	1
+ 2	9

Tens	Ones
□	
2	3
+ 3	7

Tens	Ones
□	
4	4
+ 1	6

Tens	Ones
□	
7	9
+ 1	3

Tens	Ones
1	
1	5
+ 2	7

Tens	Ones
□	
5	7
+ 3	7

Tens	Ones
□	
1	6
+ 3	5

Tens	Ones
□	
1	5
+ 4	6

Tens	Ones
□	
1	7
+ 2	4

Tens	Ones
□	
7	7
+ 1	8

Tens	Ones
□	
3	9
+ 3	5

Operations

Adding 3-Digit Numbers by Traditional Regrouping

When adding three-digit numbers, regrouping is often needed too.

Look at the example below. If the numbers in a place value column add up to more than 9 in the ones column or 99 in the tens column, we need to regroup.

Example: $545 + 269 =$ ___

First add the ones.

$5 + 9 = 14$.

14 is more than 9.
We need to regroup.

14 means 1 ten and 4 ones.

Hundreds	Tens	Ones
1	1	
5	4	5
+ 2	6	9
8	1	4

Put the 4 in the ones column
and the 1 at the top of the tens column.

Now add the tens. $10 + 40 + 60 = 110$.

110 is more than 99. We need to regroup.

Put a 1 at the bottom of the tens column to represent 10 and a 1 at the top of the hundreds column to represent 100.

Now add the hundreds. $100 + 500 + 200 = 800$.

Put your hundreds, tens, and ones together.

$800 + 10 + 4 = 814$.

The sum is 814.

Solve the equations by using traditional regrouping. Write the sums in the boxes below.

Hundreds	Tens	Ones
7	1	4
+ 2	1	7

Hundreds	Tens	Ones
2	9	5
+ 1	2	7

Hundreds	Tens	Ones
6	3	7
+ 2	9	5

Operations

Adding 3-Digit Numbers by Traditional Regrouping

Solve the equations by using traditional regrouping. Write the sums in the boxes below.

Hundreds	Tens	Ones
6	1	5
+ 1	9	5

Hundreds	Tens	Ones
3	4	7
+ 4	6	9

Hundreds	Tens	Ones
2	7	9
+ 6	1	9

Hundreds	Tens	Ones
3	1	3
+ 1	9	7

Hundreds	Tens	Ones
2	2	6
+ 4	7	4

Hundreds	Tens	Ones
1	0	5
+ 3	9	9

Hundreds	Tens	Ones
6	9	5
+ 2	2	6

Hundreds	Tens	Ones
5	8	3
+ 1	4	9

Hundreds	Tens	Ones
4	3	7
+ 3	8	9

Hundreds	Tens	Ones
5	9	4
+ 3	7	8

Hundreds	Tens	Ones
4	8	4
+ 3	8	7

Hundreds	Tens	Ones
6	0	5
+ 3	2	7

Adding 3-Digit Numbers by the Column Method

Knowing **place value** can help you solve addition equations using the **column method**.

Example:

First add each place value column and keep each sum in the correct column.

Hundreds	Tens	Ones
2	8	3
+ 6	2	9
8	10	12
9	11	2
	1	
9	1	2

The 12 in the ones column is 1 ten and 2 ones, so you need to move 1 ten to the tens place.

11 tens means you need to move 1 ten to the hundreds place.

Now the sum is:

$$283 + 629 = 912$$

Solve the equations using the column method.

Hundreds	Tens	Ones
3	6	7
+ 2	3	8

Hundreds	Tens	Ones
1	2	6
+ 4	9	5

___ + ___ = ___   ___ + ___ = ___

Operations

Adding 3-Digit Numbers by the Column Method

Solve the equations using the column method.

Hundreds	Tens	Ones
4	7	2
+ 1	4	9

___ + ___ = ___

Hundreds	Tens	Ones
1	2	8
+ 3	7	5

___ + ___ = ___

Hundreds	Tens	Ones
6	7	9
+ 2	4	5

___ + ___ = ___

Hundreds	Tens	Ones
1	3	8
+ 6	2	4

___ + ___ = ___

Operations

Subtracting 2-Digit Numbers by Traditional Regrouping

Subtracting tens and ones sometimes requires regrouping.

Look at the example below. If the top number in a place value column is smaller than the bottom number, you need to regroup.

Example: 45 - 18 = ____

First subtract the ones.

5 - 8 = ____

5 is less than 8. We need to regroup.

That means we need to take 1 set of ten

from the tens column and move it to the ones column.

Now subtract the ones. 15 - 8 = 7.

Next subtract the remaining tens. 30 - 10 = 20.

Put your tens and ones together. 20 + 7 = 27.

The difference is 27.

Tens	Ones
3	15
4̶	5̶
- 1	8
2	7

Solve the difference equations by regrouping. Write the differences below.

Tens	Ones
5	2
- 4	6

Tens	Ones
2	3
- 1	6

Tens	Ones
4	7
- 2	8

Tens	Ones
3	3
- 1	9

Tens	Ones
3	4
- 2	6

Tens	Ones
4	5
- 2	7

Tens	Ones
5	6
- 1	9

Tens	Ones
6	7
- 4	8

Operations

Subtracting 2-Digit Numbers by Traditional Regrouping

Solve the equations by regrouping. Write the differences below.

Tens	Ones
3	5
− 1	7
1	8

Tens	Ones
4	7
− 1	8
2	9

Tens	Ones
5	3
− 1	7

Tens	Ones
3	0
− 1	8

Tens	Ones
5	2
− 2	8

Tens	Ones
2	8
− 1	9

Tens	Ones
4	6
− 3	8

Tens	Ones
5	4
− 4	7

Tens	Ones
6	3
− 4	8

Tens	Ones
7	2
− 5	6

Tens	Ones
8	7
− 1	9

Tens	Ones
9	3
− 2	9

125

Operations

Subtracting 3-Digit Numbers by Traditional Regrouping

Subtracting hundreds, tens, and ones sometimes requires regrouping.

Look at the example below. If the top number in a place value column is smaller than the bottom number, you need to regroup.

Example: $853 - 584 = $ ____

First subtract the ones column.

$3 - 4 = $ ____

Hundreds	Tens	Ones
	14	
7	4̶	13
8̶	5̶	3̶
− 5	8	4
2	6	9

3 is less than 4. We need to regroup. That means take 1 set of tens from the tens column and move it to the ones column.

Now subtract the ones column.

$13 - 4 = 9$.

Next subtract the tens column.

$40 - 80 = $ ____

40 is less than 80. We need to regroup.

That means take 1 set of hundreds from the hundreds column and move it to the tens column. We now have 14 sets of 10.

Now subtract the tens column.

$140 - 80 = 60$.

Now subtract the hundreds column.

$700 - 500 = 200$.

Put your hundreds, tens, and ones together.

$200 + 60 + 9 = 269$.

The difference is 269.

Operations

Subtracting 3-Digit Numbers by Traditional Regrouping

Solve the equations by regrouping. Write the differences below.

Hundreds	Tens	Ones
6	1	0
- 4	4	7

Hundreds	Tens	Ones
7	3	1
- 1	8	6

Hundreds	Tens	Ones
7	5	4
- 1	6	8

Hundreds	Tens	Ones
6	2	3
- 2	9	5

Hundreds	Tens	Ones
6	3	3
- 5	6	7

Hundreds	Tens	Ones
3	7	3
- 2	9	6

Hundreds	Tens	Ones
9	7	2
- 3	8	3

Hundreds	Tens	Ones
6	3	2
- 1	8	5

Hundreds	Tens	Ones
9	8	2
- 3	9	4

Operations

Subtracting 3-Digit Numbers by Traditional Regrouping

Solve the equations by regrouping. Write the differences below.

Hundreds	Tens	Ones
8	3	0
− 2	4	6

Hundreds	Tens	Ones
6	3	1
− 1	5	5

Hundreds	Tens	Ones
5	3	4
− 1	4	6

Hundreds	Tens	Ones
4	3	0
− 2	7	1

Hundreds	Tens	Ones
8	1	5
− 5	6	9

Hundreds	Tens	Ones
7	3	1
− 1	7	5

Hundreds	Tens	Ones
6	6	1
− 3	7	8

Hundreds	Tens	Ones
2	3	3
− 1	7	9

Hundreds	Tens	Ones
6	3	1
− 2	8	7

Operations

1-Step Word Problems

Sometimes math equations are hidden in word problems. Read each addition or subtraction word problem carefully and write an equation that shows the unknown number. Solve your equation and write the answer on the line.

Example: Ella makes bracelets for her friends and family. She had 89 but gave some away. She has 56 bracelets left. How many did she give away?

$89 - ? = 56$ $89 - 56 = 33$

Ella gave away <u>33</u> bracelets.

Oscar collects miniature race cars. He has 29 cars. His friend Caleb has 15 more cars than Oscar. How many cars does Caleb have?

Caleb has _____ cars.

Finn loves the space shuttle. He knows it is 122 feet long and 78 feet wide. How much longer is the space shuttle than it is wide?

The shuttle is _____ feet longer than it is wide.

Operations

1-Step Word Problems

Solve the 1-step word problems. Show your thinking by writing your equations and solving them to find the answers.

Monica sells kayaks. She has sold 27 of them to a group of vacationers. There are still 49 kayaks in her shop. How many kayaks did Monica have when she opened her shop?

Sam is a firefighter. He has 42 firefighter friends working at his station. Then 26 of them move to another fire station. How many firefighters are left at Sam's station?

Jack is setting up 26 tents at his campground. He has already finished setting up 18 tents. How many tents still need to be set up?

Katie has 79 tomato seedlings to plant on her family farm. She has planted 38 seedlings so far. How many tomato seedlings does Katie have left to plant?

Rectangular Arrays

Determine how many rows and columns there are for each array of objects.

____ rows by ____ columns   ____ rows by ____ columns

Both arrays have ____ ladybugs.

____ rows by ____ columns   ____ rows by ____ columns

Both arrays have ____ smiley faces.

____ rows by ____ columns   ____ rows by ____ columns

Both arrays have ____ sea stars.

134

2-Step Word Problems

To solve word problems with two steps, you need to figure out what operations you will need to use for each step. You may need to:

| add/add | add/subtract |
| subtract/subtract | subtract/add |

Example: Molly buys 4 shirts and 5 skirts. She returns 2 skirts the next day. How many pieces of clothing did Molly keep?

First step: 4 shirts + 5 skirts = 9 pieces of clothing

Second step: 9 pieces – 2 skirts = 7 pieces of clothing

Molly kept _7_ pieces of clothing.

Solve the 2-step word problems. Show your thinking by writing the equations and solving for each step.

There were 20 people on the bus. Then 4 people got off at the next stop. Later, 8 people got on at the last stop. How many people are on the bus when it arrives at the station?

First step: Second step:

Hayley's mom made 26 cupcakes for Hayley's birthday party. Hayley made 10 more. Then Hayley's sister came in and ate 4 cupcakes! Does Hayley have enough cupcakes to serve 30 friends at her party?

First step: Second step:

Circle the answer: Yes, Hayley has enough cupcakes.

No, Hayley does not have enough cupcakes.

2-Step Word Problems

Solve the 2-step word problems. Show your thinking by writing the equations and solving for each step.

There are 18 baseballs and 13 volleyballs in the locker room. There are 10 balls used during practice after school. How many balls are left in the locker room?

First step: Second step:

The pet store has 46 fish in a large tank and 23 fish in a smaller tank. A lady buys 14 fish in the morning. How many fish does the pet store have now?

First step: Second step:

Marcus had 52 markers. He received 12 more as a gift. Then he lost 17 of them at school. Does he have more markers or less markers than he originally had?

First step: Second step:

Circle the answer: Marcus has MORE markers.
                     Marcus has FEWER markers.

Rectangular Arrays

A **rectangular array** is an arrangement of objects in rows and columns in equal groups. Each **row** has the same number of objects, and each **column** has the same number of objects.

Example:

__2__ rows by __4__ columns   __4__ rows by __2__ columns

Both arrays have __8__ circles.

Determine how many rows and columns there are for each array of objects.

Good job! 9/10

__4__ rows by __3__ columns   __3__ rows by __4__ columns

Both arrays have __Z__ stars. X

✓

__2__ rows by __2__ columns   __2__ rows by __2__ columns

Both arrays have __4__ flowers.

Understanding Multiplication

Creating Equations

You can find out "how many" by combining the same number, or equal groups, of the same number.

Example: 3 groups of 5 is $5 + 5 + 5 = 15$ or $3 \times 5 = 15$

 = 15

Solve the equations by combining the groups. Write the numbers on the lines below.

2 groups of 3

$\underline{3} + \underline{3} = \underline{6}$

$\underline{2} \times 3 = \underline{6}$

3 groups of 3

___ + ___ + ___ = ___

___ x 3 = ___

3 groups of 4

___ + ___ + ___ = ___

___ x 4 = ___

4 groups of 5

___ + ___ + ___ + ___ = ___

___ x 5 = ___

2 groups of 5

___ + ___ = ___

___ x 5 = ___

2 groups of 4

___ + ___ = ___

___ x 4 = ___

Understanding Multiplication

Creating Equations

Use the groups to help solve the equations. Write the numbers on the lines below.

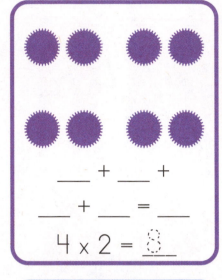

___ + ___ +

___ + ___ = ___

4 x 2 = 8

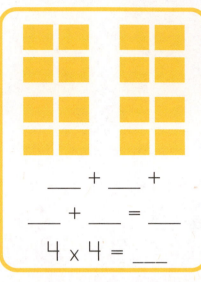

___ + ___ +

___ + ___ = ___

4 x 4 = ___

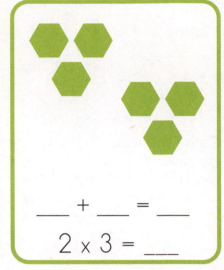

___ + ___ = ___

2 x 3 = ___

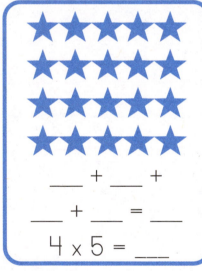

___ + ___ +

___ + ___ = ___

4 x 5 = ___

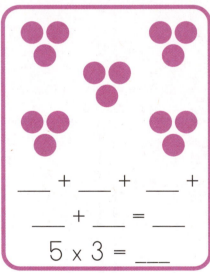

___ + ___ + ___ +

___ + ___ = ___

5 x 3 = ___

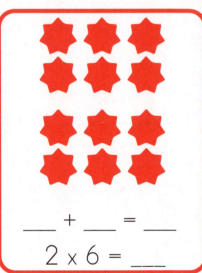

___ + ___ = ___

2 x 6 = ___

___ + ___ + ___ +

___ + ___ + ___ = ___

6 x 3 = ___

___ + ___ = ___

2 x 7 = ___

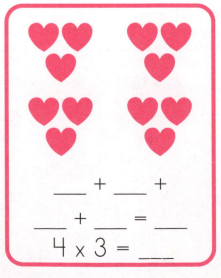

___ + ___ +

___ + ___ = ___

4 x 3 = ___

Regular and Irregular Shapes

Regular and Irregular Shapes

A regular shape has all equal sides and all equal angles. An irregular shape has at least one side that is a different length than its other sides and/or at least one different angle than its other angles.

Example:

regular pentagon

irregular pentagon

Circle the correct type for each shape.

TRIANGLE

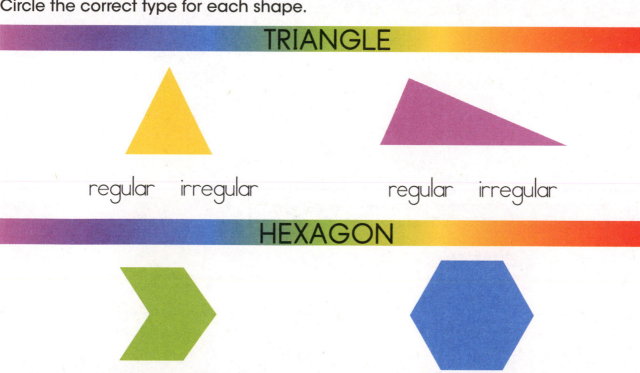

regular   irregular

regular   irregular

HEXAGON

regular   irregular

regular   irregular

OCTAGON

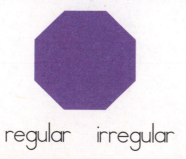

regular   irregular

regular   irregular

Regular and Irregular Shapes

Regular and Irregular Shapes

Circle the correct type for each shape.

QUADRILATERAL

regular   irregular

regular   irregular

PENTAGON

regular   irregular

regular   irregular

HEPTAGON

regular   irregular

regular   irregular

DECAGON

regular   irregular

regular   irregular

One Half

One half means a figure is partitioned into **2 equal shares**.

Example: one whole   **1 out of 2 equal shares** or **one half**

Shade 1 out of 2 equal shares for each shape. Write the missing information below each shape.

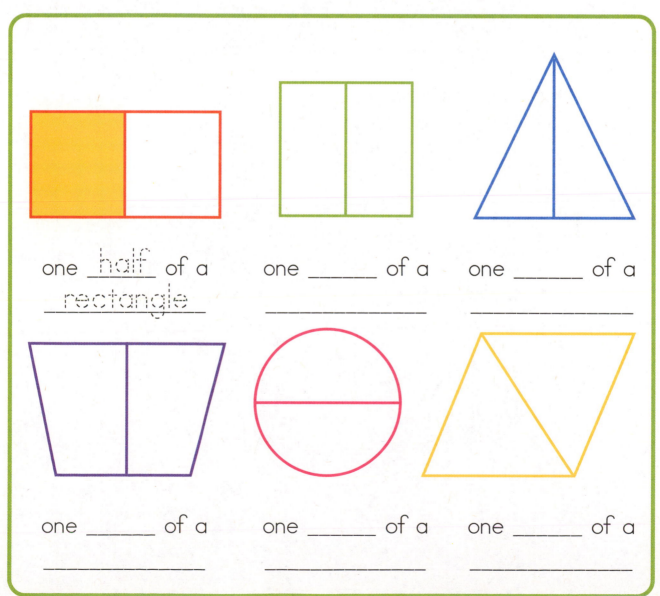

one __half__ of a
__rectangle__

one _____ of a
_____

one _____ of a
_____

one _____ of a
_____

one _____ of a
_____

one _____ of a
_____

139

Shapes and Shares

One Third

One third means a figure is partitioned into **3 equal shares**.

Example: one whole   1 out of 3 equal shares **or** one third

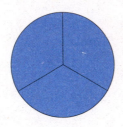 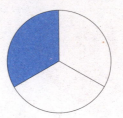

Shade 1 out of 3 equal shares for each shape. Write the missing information below each shape.

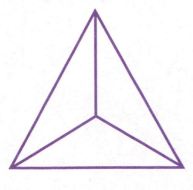

one <u>third</u> of a
<u>rectangle</u>

one _____ of a
_____

one _____ of a
_____

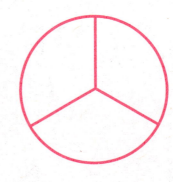

one _____ of a
_____

one _____ of a
_____

One Fourth

One fourth means a figure is partitioned into **4 equal shares**.

Example: one whole   1 out of 4 equal shares **or** one fourth

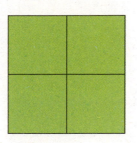

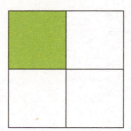

Shade 1 out of 4 equal shares for each shape. Write the missing information below each shape.

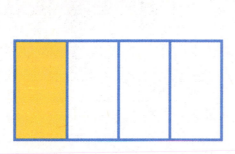

one ___fourth___ of a ___rectangle___

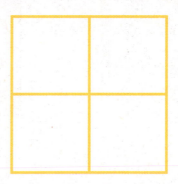

one _____ of a _____

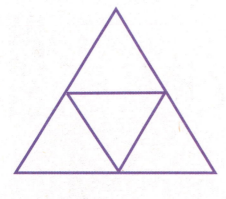

one _____ of a _____

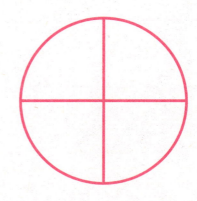

one _____ of a _____

Area

Area is the **amount of surface space inside** a flat figure.

Example: All three figures have the same area.

____4____ square units

Write how many square units each object has in its area.

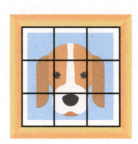   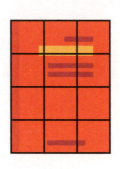   

_____ square units   _____ square units   _____ square units

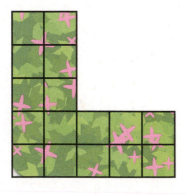   

_____ square units   _____ square unit   _____ square units

142

Measurement

Measuring Customary Length

Inches are used to measure **small things**.

Example: The feather is **8 inches** long.

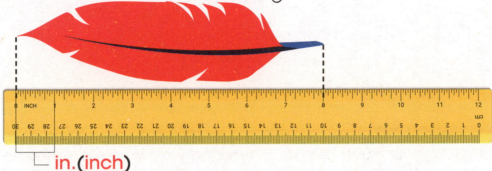

in. (inch)

Use the rulers to measure each item in inches. Write the measurements on the lines below.

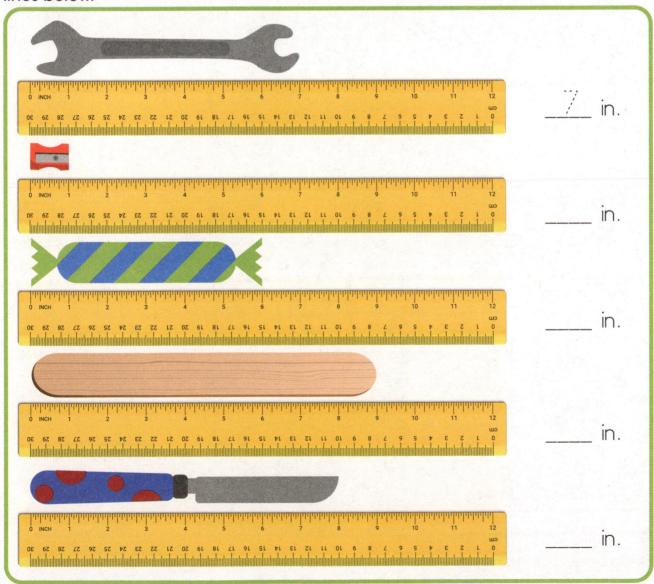

_7_ in.

_____ in.

_____ in.

_____ in.

_____ in.

Measurement

Measuring Customary Length

An **estimate** is an **educated guess**. Sometimes we need to make an educated guess about how long something is.

Example:

The nail is about 1 inch long.

in.(inch)

Estimate the length of each item in inches and write your estimates on the lines in the first column below. Then use a ruler to measure the pictures of each item and write the exact measurements on the lines in the second column below.

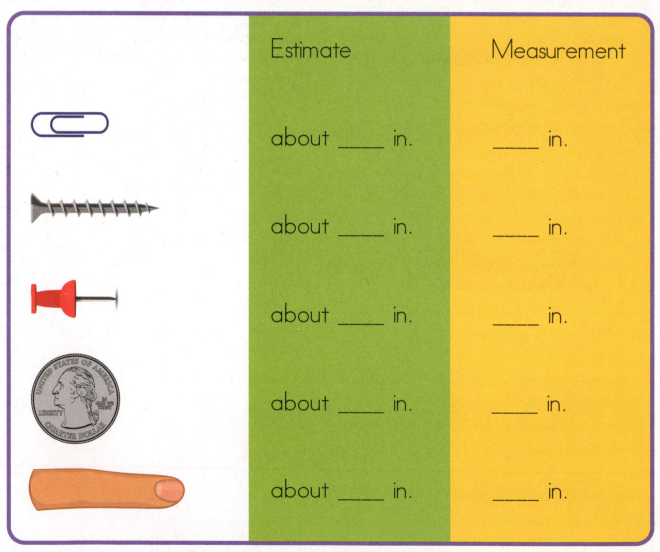

	Estimate	Measurement
	about ____ in.	____ in.
	about ____ in.	____ in.
	about ____ in.	____ in.
	about ____ in.	____ in.
	about ____ in.	____ in.

Find some more things around your house to measure with your ruler!

Measuring Metric Length

Centimeters are used to measure **small things**.

Example: The feather is 20 cm long.

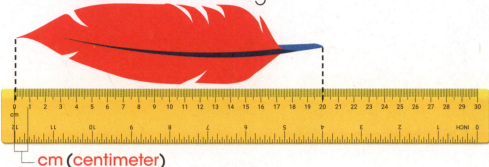

cm (centimeter)

Use the rulers to measure each item in centimeters. Write the measurements on the lines below.

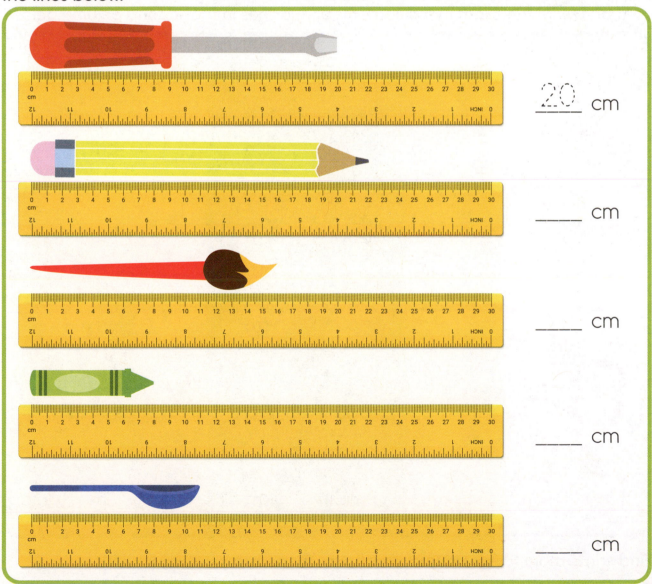

20 cm

_____ cm

_____ cm

_____ cm

_____ cm

Measurement

Measuring Metric Length

An estimate is an educated guess. Sometimes we need to make an educated guess about how long something is.

Example:

The dime is about 2 cm long.

cm (centimeter)

Estimate the length of each item in centimeters and write your estimates on the lines in the first column below. Then use a ruler to measure the pictures of each item and write the exact measurements on the lines in the second column below.

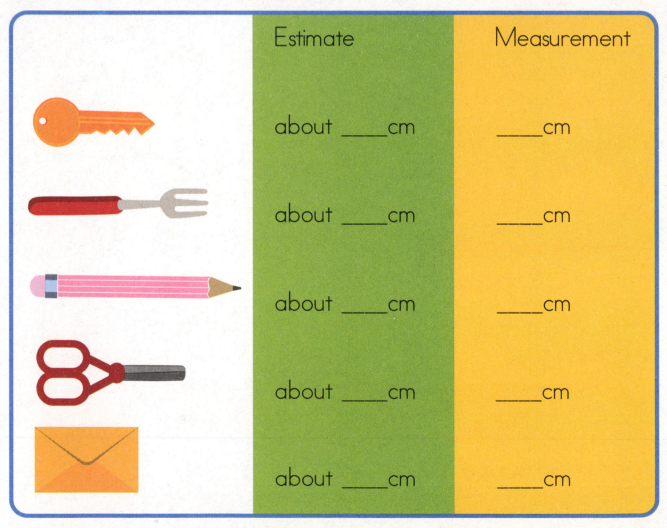

	Estimate	Measurement
key	about _____ cm	_____ cm
fork	about _____ cm	_____ cm
pencil	about _____ cm	_____ cm
scissors	about _____ cm	_____ cm
envelope	about _____ cm	_____ cm

Find some more things around your house to measure with your ruler!

Time

Measuring Time to the Quarter Hour

Every 15 minutes is one quarter of an hour.

When the **minute hand is on the 3**, it is
15 minutes past or **a quarter past the hour.**

When the **minute hand is on the 6**,
it is **30 minutes past** or **half past the hour.**

When the **minute hand is on the 9**,
it is **45 minutes past** or **a quarter to the next hour.**

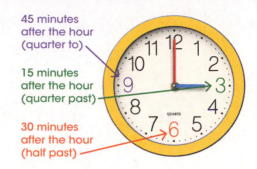

45 minutes after the hour (quarter to)

15 minutes after the hour (quarter past)

30 minutes after the hour (half past)

Write the time under the clocks below.

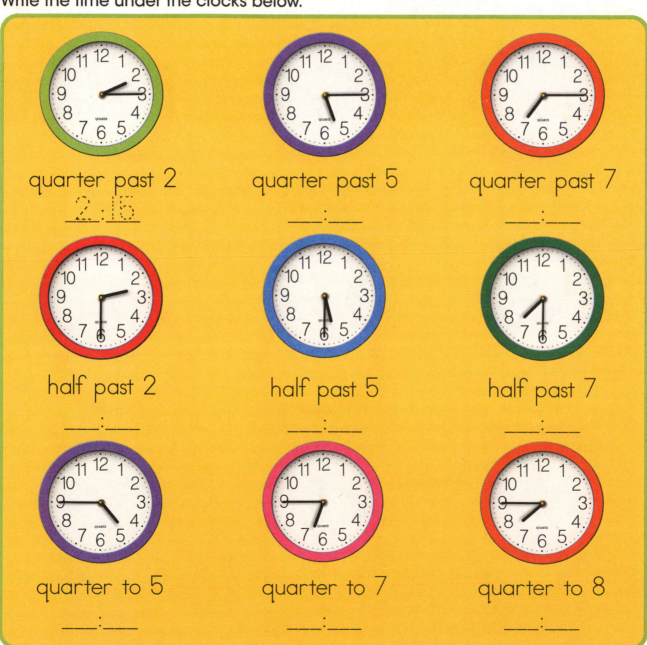

quarter past 2

2 : 15

quarter past 5

___:___

quarter past 7

___:___

half past 2

___:___

half past 5

___:___

half past 7

___:___

quarter to 5

___:___

quarter to 7

___:___

quarter to 8

___:___

147

Time to Five Minutes

What time is it? Write the time under each clock.

2:05

What time is it? Draw the hands on the clocks to match the digital times.

8:05   1:10   5:35

4:45   6:25   3:40

Time

Time to Five Minutes

Draw a line from the digital clock to its matching analog clock.

Time

A.M. and P.M.

Events happening **before** 12 noon are called **a.m.** events. Events happening **after** 12 noon are called **p.m.** events.

When are these events happening? Circle a.m. or p.m. below each picture.

150

Money

Writing Money Amounts

When writing dollar and cent amounts, a decimal point is placed in between the whole dollars and remaining cents.

Example:

$10.03

Don't forget! If the remaining cents equal less than 10 cents, you need to put a 0 in the tens place.

Add up the money, then write the dollar and cent amounts on the lines below.

$11.50

_____

_____

_____

_____

_____

Writing Money Amounts

9/10 nice JOB

Add up the money, then write the dollar and cent amounts on the lines below.

25.03 ✓

15.07 ✓

6.21 6.22

2.08 ✓

11.31 ✓

6.75 ✓

12.50 ✓

30.41 ✓

Writing Money Amounts

Subtract the money with an X on it, then write the equations and totals on the lines below.

Example:

$$\$20.60 - \$5.10 = \ ^\$15.50$$

_____

_____

_____

_____

Money

Solving Money Word Problems

Read the word problems and then write an equation to help you find the missing amounts.

Example: Susie had some money in her piggy bank from last week. Today, she earned $5.50 for her weekly chores. Now she has $10.25 in her bank. How much did she have in her bank last week?

$? + {}^\$5.50 = {}^\$10.25$

${}^\$10.25 - {}^\$5.50 = {}^\$4.75$

Susie had ${}^\$4.75$ in her piggy bank last week.

Jim walks into a store. He has ${}^\$10.00$ to spend. He buys a blue shirt. When he leaves the store, he has ${}^\$5.25$ left. How much did his shirt cost?

Candice earned $8.35 for singing at a party. She earned $7.55 for singing at another party. How much money does she have now?

Terri went to the same store as Jim. She had ${}^\$15.25$ to spend. How much more money does she have to spend than Jim did when he first went into the store?

Data Management

Reading a Picture Graph

A picture graph uses pictures to represent units. The key tells you the unit quantity.

Flowers for Friends

Key: = 1 Flower

Josh	
Toby	
Leo	
Donna	
Claudia	

Use the picture graph to answer the questions about the data. Write your answers on the lines below.

How many more flowers does Josh have than Toby? _____

How many flowers do Leo and Claudia have combined? _____

How many fewer flowers does Leo have than Donna? _____

How many flowers do the friends have if they put all their

flowers in one vase? _____

Reading a Line Plot

A **line plot** represents the **frequency of amounts in a group**.

Example: Egg Hunt

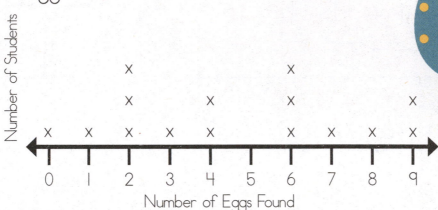

The line plot tells you that no students out of 15 found 5 eggs. Three students found 6 eggs. One student found zero eggs.

Answer the questions using the line plot. Write your answers on the lines below.

Mr. Smith's gym class was asked to do push-ups without resting. Here are the results:

Push-Up Contest

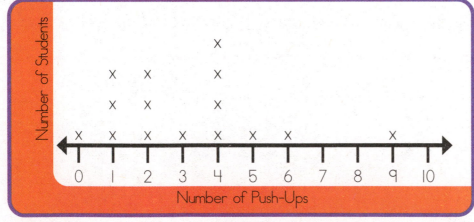

How many students were able to do 5 push-ups? _____

How many students could do one push-up? _____

What numbers of push-ups did no students do? _____ _____ _____

What numbers of push-ups were done by three students? _____ _____

Data Management

Creating a Line Plot

Transfer the collected tally chart data to the line plot below using Xs.

Students with Pets

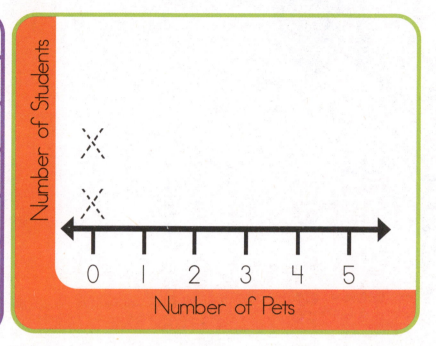

Tally Chart

Pets	Students
0	II
1	III
2	HHT
3	III
4	I
5	

Line Plot

Answer the questions below. Write your answers on the lines.

How many students own less than 2 pets? _____

How many students own more than 2 pets? _____

How many pets are owned by three students? _____ _____

157

CERTIFICATE
of Achievement

....

has successfully completed
2nd Grade Math

Date:

Signed:

Extra Practice Pages

Table of Contents

ABC Order

Put the words below in alphabetical order.

rooster   apple   violin   cat

antelope   television

butter   tennis   hockey   hose

1.

2.

3.

4.

5.

1.

2.

3.

4.

5.

Blends and Sounds

Read the sentences below and use the pictures to help you fill in the missing letters in the words to show the consonant blends.

I can use a ___ ___obe.

My favorite color is ___ ___ue.

I love my cozy ___ ___anket.

I found a four-leaf ___ ___ over.

Look at the ___ ___ouds in the sky.

Blends and Sounds

Say the names of the pictures and fill in the missing letters in the words to show the beginning consonant blends.

__ __ een

__ __ ade

__ __ ink

__ __ ayon

__ __ etzel

__ __ ice

Blends and Sounds

Say the names of the pictures and fill in the missing letters in the words to show the ending consonant blends.

sta___ ___

wi___ ___

a ___ ___

ha___ ___

sto___ ___

pai___ ___

Blends and Sounds

Fill in the missing letters and color the pictures with the **ph** sounds.

al ____ abet

geogra ____ y

ne ____ ew

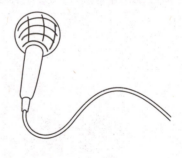

micro ____ one

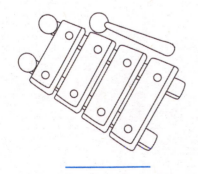

xylo ____ one

ele ____ ant

Blends and Sounds

Fill in the missing letters and color the pictures with the **kn** sounds.

door____ob

____ight

____eel

____uckle

____owledge

un____own

Blends and Sounds

Fill in the missing letters and color the pictures with the er sounds.

socc _____

flow _____

wat _____

Fill in the missing letters and color the pictures with the ir sounds.

g _____ l

c _____ cle

st _____

Fill in the missing letters and color the pictures with the ur sounds.

f _____

s _____ f

p _____ se

Digraphs

Say the names of the pictures and listen for the digraph sound. Fill in the missing digraphs for each word below.

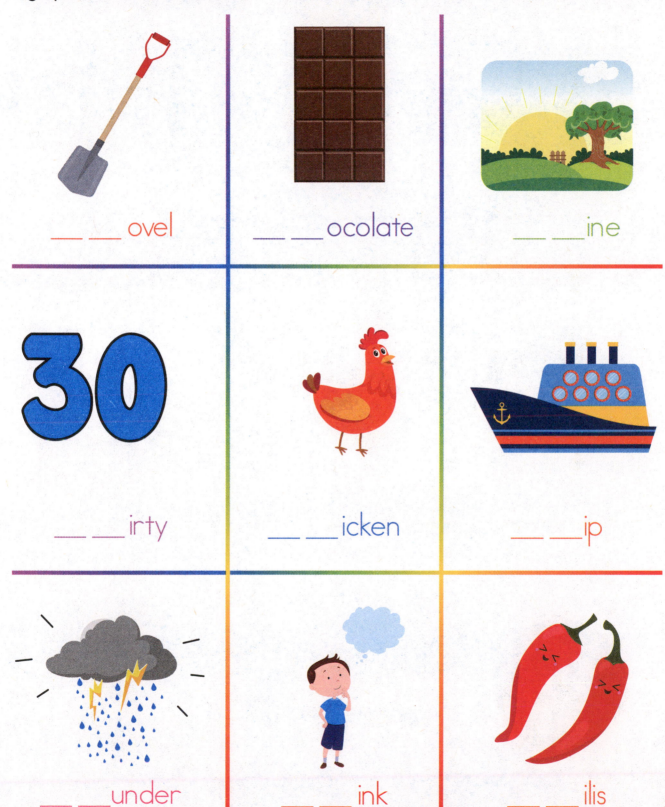

___ ___ovel

___ ___ocolate

___ ___ine

___ ___irty

___ ___icken

___ ___ip

___ ___under

___ ___ink

___ ___ilis

Digraphs

Say the names of the pictures and listen for the digraph sound. Fill in the digraphs for each word below.

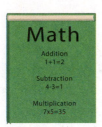

ma___ ___

fini___ ___

lun___ ___

blu___ ___

ostri___ ___

lea___ ___

bla___ ___

tru___ ___

bran___ ___

Short Vowels

Read the words on the kites below and listen for the vowel sound. Then write the words in the correct short vowel category in the chart below.

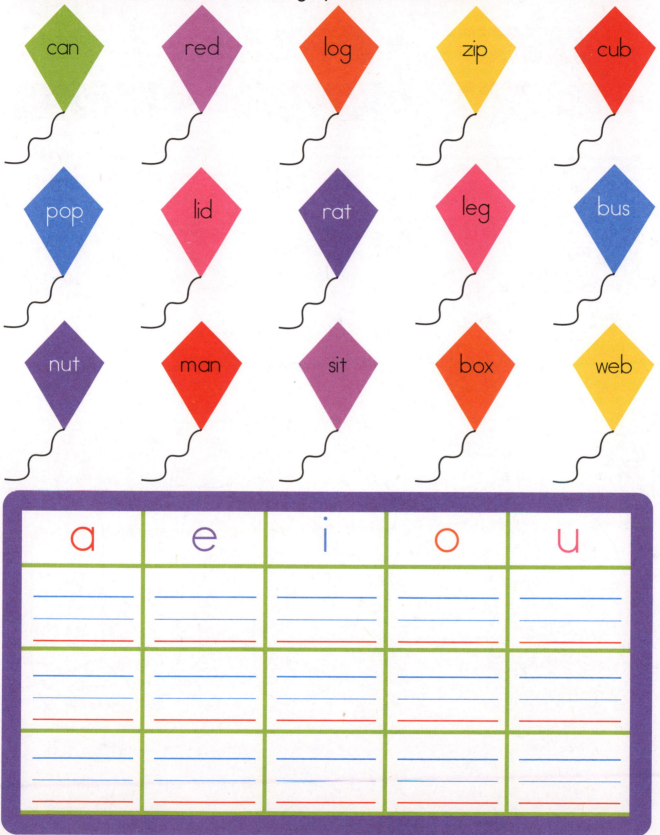

Short Vowels

Read the short vowel words in the picture below. Listen for the vowel sound. Then color the short vowel words using the color code below.

short a

short e

short i

short o

short u

☺

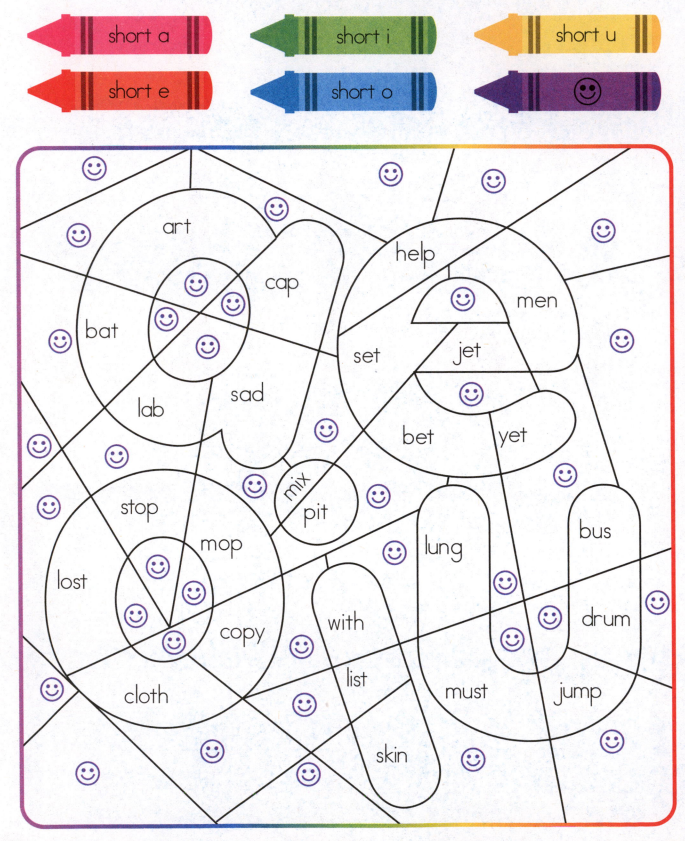

Long Vowels

Look at the pictures and fill in the correct long **a** sound below.

spr____

M____

tr____n

gr____

n____l

r____n

s____

ch____n

st____rs

Long Vowels

Look at the pictures and fill in the correct long **e** sound below.

sh____t

____gle

p____ch

b____k

ch____k

b____ch

tr____

d____r

b____n

Long Vowels

Look at the pictures and fill in the correct long **i** sound below.

l___t

b___ke

qu___t

fl___t

cr___

d___ce

n___t

r___t

s___t

Long Vowels

Look at the pictures and fill in the correct long **o** sound below.

b____rd

r____

b____l

t____d

thr____

l____f

r____r

____tmeal

g____

Long Vowels

Read the long vowel words in the picture below. Listen for the vowel sound.
Then color the long vowel words using the color code below.

long a long e long i long o long u ☺

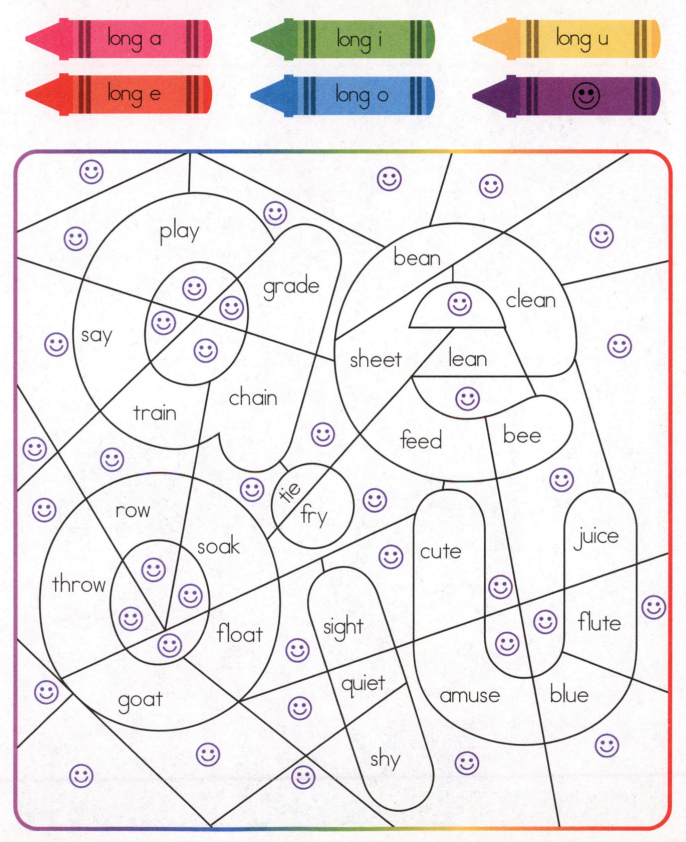

Short and Long Vowels

Short and Long Vowels

Read the words in the bubbles. Color the short vowel words red and the long vowel words blue.

Sight Word Practice

Look at the scene. Create an event and write about it on the lines below. Use sight words you have learned to describe what is happening in the scene.

Nouns

Read the rhymes below and circle the **common** nouns.

Meg Yorke
eats an egg with a fork.

Big Matt
hits the ball with a bat.

Hayley the clown
is wearing a crown.

My dog, Applejack,
stole my snack.

My friend Skye
baked me a pie.

A girl named Cass
drinks out of a glass.

Nouns

Read the rhymes below and circle the proper nouns.

My friend Lamar
likes to play guitar.

Uncle Lars
drives very fast cars.

Jake likes to make
his favorite cupcake.

Doctor Ray gave me a shot,
and it left a little dot.

My best friend, Shawn,
fed the swan.

My family went to the pool
with Mr. O'Doul.

Adjectives

Draw a picture of a dog in the box below. Use your imagination!

Use adjectives to answer the questions about your dog on the lines below.

What size is your dog?

What color is your dog?

What kind of personality does your dog have?

List some other words that describe your dog.

Adjectives

Read the sentences below and circle the adjectives in each sentence.

The brown dog jumped over the big fence.

The marshmallows are soft and chewy.

I got a new summer skirt.

It is hot and dry outside today.

I love my cuddly blue teddy bear.

Look at the shiny gold crown!

Synonyms and Antonyms

Read each sentence below and circle the synonym of the highlighted word.

The towel is wet.   damp   dry   hot

The dog is fast.   short   clean   quick

The flower is pretty.   hard   beautiful   strong

Read each sentence below and circle the antonym of the highlighted word.

The truck is loud.   slow   red   quiet

The boy is short.   smart   tall   sad

The snail is slow.   dry   fast   clean

Suffixes

Read the words below and add the suffixes er and est to make new words with new meanings.

smart   bright   sweet   soft   quiet

er	est

Compound Words

Look at the mittens below. Each one has a word on it. Match the mittens with words that go together to make a compound word. Write the compound words below and draw a picture for each one to match their new meanings.

Look at the illustration below and read the labels.

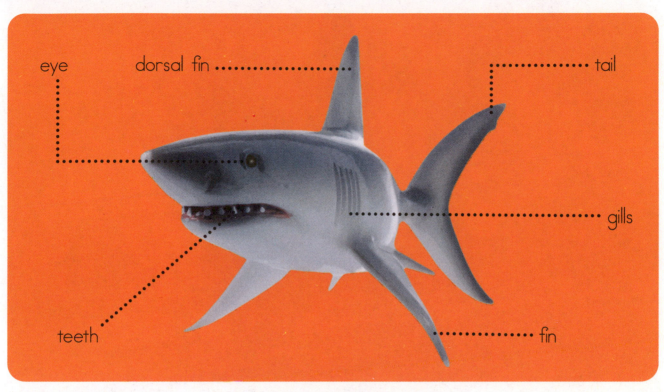

eye   dorsal fin ············· tail

gills

teeth   fin

Use the labels to help you answer the questions below.

How many dorsal fins does a shark have?

_____

_____

What is on the side of the shark?

_____

_____

What other things did you learn from the labels?

_____

_____

_____

Farms are full of many different types of animals. Each animal is unique. Cows can provide milk, and sheep can provide wool.

Use the illustration and caption above to help you answer the questions below.

Describe what you see in the illustration.

_____

_____

_____

What does the caption tell you about the illustration?

_____

_____

_____

Practice writing the uppercase and lowercase cursive letters on the lines below.

Practice writing the uppercase and lowercase cursive letters on the lines below.

Cc

Dd

C

c

D

d

Pencil Practice

Practice writing the uppercase and lowercase cursive letters on the lines below.

Pencil Practice

Practice writing the uppercase and lowercase cursive letters on the lines below.

Gg

Hh

Practice writing the uppercase and lowercase cursive letters on the lines below.

Pencil Practice

Practice writing the uppercase and lowercase cursive letters on the lines below.

Pencil Practice

Practice writing the uppercase and lowercase cursive letters on the lines below.

193

Pencil Practice

Practice writing the uppercase and lowercase cursive letters on the lines below.

194

Pencil Practice

Practice writing the uppercase and lowercase cursive letters on the lines below.

Pencil Practice

Practice writing the uppercase and lowercase cursive letters on the lines below.

Pencil Practice

Practice writing the uppercase and lowercase cursive letters on the lines below.

Pencil Practice

Practice writing the uppercase and lowercase cursive letters on the lines below.

Ww Xx

$\mathcal{W}$

w

$\mathcal{X}$

x

Pencil Practice

Practice writing the uppercase and lowercase cursive letters on the lines below.

Comparing Numbers

Look at the numbers below and put the correct symbol in the middle of the two numbers to show if the number is greater than >, less than <, or equal to = the second number.

333 331

642 634

734 754

889 898

702 632

433 343

471 451

907 907

Comparing Numbers

Look at the numbers below and circle the correct comparison phrase in the middle of the two numbers.

180 is | greater than / less than / equal to | 400

111 is | greater than / less than / equal to | 111

161 is | greater than / less than / equal to | 171

626 is | greater than / less than / equal to | 262

201 is | greater than / less than / equal to | 201

414 is | greater than / less than / equal to | 414

110 is | greater than / less than / equal to | 111

201 is | greater than / less than / equal to | 210

910 is | greater than / less than / equal to | 810

754 is | greater than / less than / equal to | 745

442 is | greater than / less than / equal to | 244

777 is | greater than / less than / equal to | 777

Place Value

Put the following numbers in order from greatest to least.

488, 484, 844

_____ , _____ , _____

337, 733, 373

_____ , _____ , _____

594, 194, 694

_____ , _____ , _____

222, 111, 101

_____ , _____ , _____

776, 777, 779

_____ , _____ , _____

123, 321, 213

_____ , _____ , _____

Place Value

Put the following numbers in order from least to greatest.

352, 125, 501

_____ , _____ , _____

623, 603, 671

_____ , _____ , _____

901, 989, 931

_____ , _____ , _____

438, 223, 639

_____ , _____ , _____

222, 202, 220

_____ , _____ , _____

521, 512, 152

_____ , _____ , _____

Read the math stories and answer the questions.

Farmer John loves his farm animals. He has barns with 100 animals, pens with 10 animals, and a few animals who wander the farm.

How many animals does Farmer John have? _____

Peggy bakes pies. She has trucks filled with 100 pies, boxes filled with 10 pies, and some pies leftover.

How many pies does Peggy have? _____

Place Value

Read the math stories and answer the questions.

Sammy loves to write letters. He has boxes filled with 100 stamps, piles of 10 stamps, and a few stamps left over.

How many stamps does Sammy have? _____

Luke loves his blocks. He has bins filled with 100 blocks, baskets with 10 blocks, and some other blocks on the floor.

How many blocks does Luke have? _____

Fractions

Shade 1 out of 2 equal shares for each shape. Write the missing information below each shape.

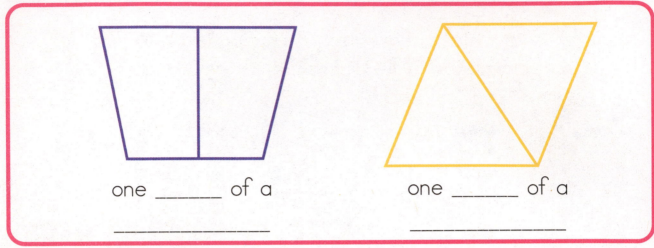

one _____ of a

_____

one _____ of a

_____

Shade 1 out of 3 equal shares for each shape. Write the missing information below each shape.

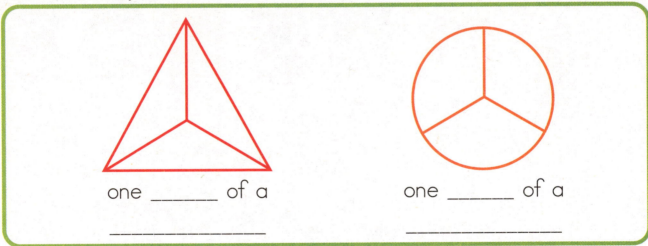

one _____ of a

_____

one _____ of a

_____

Shade 1 out of 4 equal shares for each shape. Write the missing information below each shape.

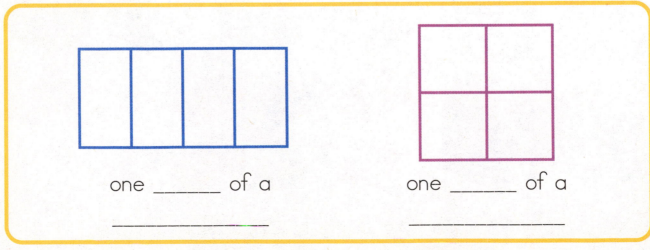

one _____ of a

_____

one _____ of a

_____

Understanding Multiplication

Solve the equations by combining the groups. Write the numbers on the lines below.

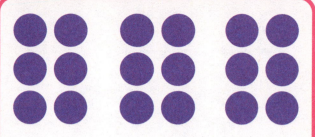

3 groups of 6

___ + ___ + ___ = ___

___ x 6 = ___

2 groups of 4

___ + ___ = ___

___ x 4 = ___

2 groups of 5

___ + ___ = ___

___ x 5 = ___

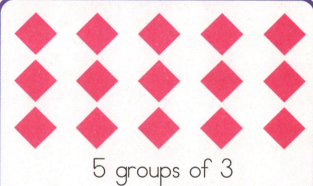

5 groups of 3

___ + ___ + ___ + ___ + ___ = ___

___ x 3 = ___

2 groups of 6

___ + ___ = ___

___ x 6 = ___

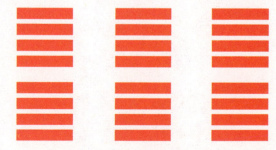

6 groups of 4

___ + ___ + ___ + ___ + ___ + ___ = ___

___ x 4 = ___

Understanding Multiplication

Solve the equations by combining the groups. Write the numbers on the lines below.

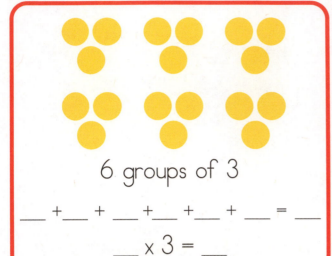

6 groups of 3

__ + __ + __ + __ + __ + __ = __

__ x 3 = __

5 groups of 4

__ + __ + __ + __ + __ = __

__ x 4 = __

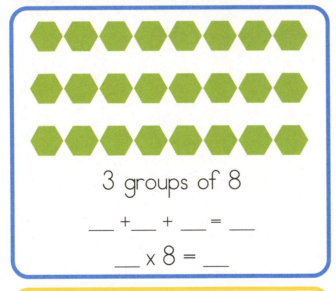

3 groups of 8

__ + __ + __ = __

__ x 8 = __

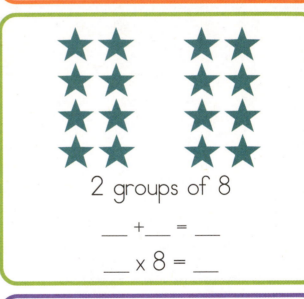

2 groups of 8

__ + __ = __

__ x 8 = __

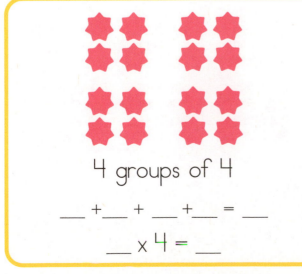

4 groups of 4

__ + __ + __ + __ = __

__ x 4 = __

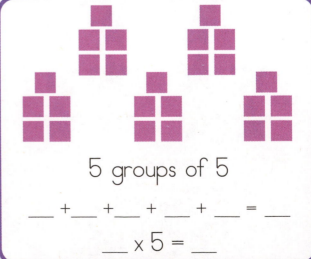

5 groups of 5

__ + __ + __ + __ + __ = __

__ x 5 = __

Rectangular Arrays

Determine how many rows and columns there are for each array of objects.

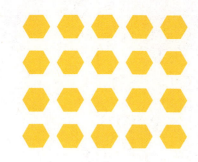

____ rows by ____ columns   ____ rows by ____ columns

Both arrays have ____ hexagons.

____ rows by ____ columns   ____ rows by ____ columns

Both arrays have ____ stars.

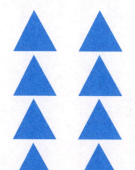

____ rows by ____ columns   ____ rows by ____ columns

Both arrays have ____ triangles.

Operations

Solve the equations by regrouping. Write the sums in the boxes below.

Tens	Ones
☐	
4	9
+ 1	8

Tens	Ones
☐	
2	6
+ 1	7

Tens	Ones
☐	
4	7
+ 3	5

Tens	Ones
☐	
7	4
+ 1	7

Tens	Ones
☐	
1	9
+ 2	7

Tens	Ones
☐	
1	1
+ 2	9

Tens	Ones
☐	
2	3
+ 3	7

Tens	Ones
☐	
4	4
+ 1	6

Tens	Ones
☐	
7	9
+ 1	3

Tens	Ones
☐	
1	5
+ 2	7

Tens	Ones
☐	
5	7
+ 3	7

Tens	Ones
☐	
1	6
+ 3	5

Tens	Ones
☐	
1	5
+ 4	6

Tens	Ones
☐	
1	7
+ 2	4

Tens	Ones
☐	
7	7
+ 1	8

Tens	Ones
☐	
3	9
+ 3	5

Operations

Solve the equations by using traditional regrouping. Write the sums in the boxes below.

Hundreds	Tens	Ones
6	1	5
+ 1	9	5

Hundreds	Tens	Ones
3	4	7
+ 4	6	9

Hundreds	Tens	Ones
2	7	9
+ 6	1	9

Hundreds	Tens	Ones
3	1	3
+ 1	9	7

Hundreds	Tens	Ones
2	2	6
+ 4	7	4

Hundreds	Tens	Ones
1	0	5
+ 3	9	9

Hundreds	Tens	Ones
6	9	5
+ 2	2	6

Hundreds	Tens	Ones
5	8	3
+ 1	4	9

Hundreds	Tens	Ones
4	3	7
+ 3	8	9

Hundreds	Tens	Ones
5	9	4
+ 3	7	8

Hundreds	Tens	Ones
4	8	4
+ 3	8	7

Hundreds	Tens	Ones
6	0	5
+ 3	2	7

Operations

Solve the equations using the column method. Write the equations and the sums on the lines below.

Hundreds	Tens	Ones
4	7	2
+ 1	4	9

_____ + _____ = _____

Hundreds	Tens	Ones
1	2	8
+ 3	7	5

_____ + _____ = _____

Hundreds	Tens	Ones
6	7	9
+ 2	4	5

_____ + _____ = _____

Hundreds	Tens	Ones
1	3	8
+ 6	2	4

_____ + _____ = _____

Operations

Solve the equations by regrouping. Write the differences below.

Tens	Ones
3	5
− 1	7

Tens	Ones
4	7
− 1	8

Tens	Ones
5	3
− 1	7

Tens	Ones
3	0
− 1	8

Tens	Ones
5	2
− 2	8

Tens	Ones
2	8
− 1	9

Tens	Ones
4	6
− 3	8

Tens	Ones
5	4
− 4	7

Tens	Ones
8	1
− 2	7

Tens	Ones
7	2
− 5	6

Tens	Ones
8	7
− 1	9

Tens	Ones
9	4
− 7	7

Tens	Ones
7	3
− 4	9

Tens	Ones
6	4
− 5	8

Tens	Ones
9	2
− 3	8

Tens	Ones
7	4
− 5	6

Operations

Solve the equations by regrouping. Write the differences below.

Hundreds	Tens	Ones
6	1	0
- 4	4	7

Hundreds	Tens	Ones
7	3	1
- 1	8	6

Hundreds	Tens	Ones
7	5	4
- 1	6	8

Hundreds	Tens	Ones
6	2	3
- 2	9	5

Hundreds	Tens	Ones
6	3	3
- 5	6	7

Hundreds	Tens	Ones
3	7	3
- 2	9	6

Hundreds	Tens	Ones
9	7	2
- 3	8	3

Hundreds	Tens	Ones
6	3	2
- 1	8	5

Hundreds	Tens	Ones
9	8	2
- 3	9	4

Time

Look at the digital clocks below. Draw a line from each digital clock to the matching analog clock.

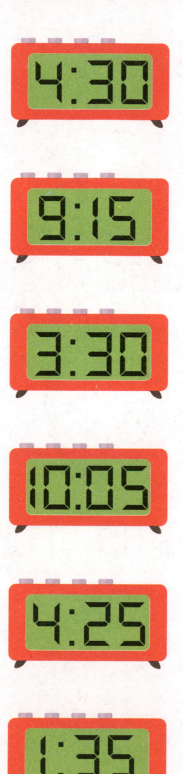

Time

Read the analog clocks and circle the matching digital times.

4:30 11:30 2:30 3:15 5:30 4:30

9:30 10:30 4:45 5:35 3:00 7:00

5:30 2:30 7:15 9:30 11:30 12:00

Time

Read the digital time and circle the correct analog clock.

Money

Add up the money, then write the dollar and cent amounts on the lines below.

_____   _____

_____   _____

_____   _____

_____   _____

218

Money

Add up the money, then write the dollar and cent amounts on the lines below.

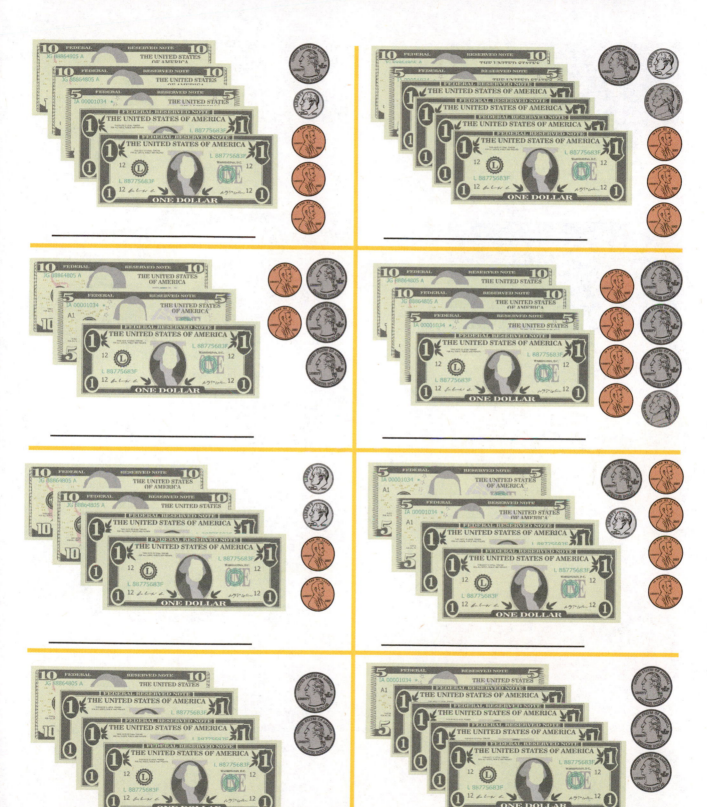

Count the money and draw a line to match each set to the correct amount.

$4.25

$3.50

$9.00

$5.35

$6.85

Data Management

Class Fruit

Use the picture graph to answer the questions and write the answers on the lines below.

How many strawberries does Grace have? _____

How many bananas does Anne have? _____

How many pieces of fruit do Billy and Anna have altogether? _____

How many pieces of fruit do Grace and Jake have altogether? _____

How many pieces of fruit do the friends have in all? _____

Data Management

We Love to Paint

Use the picture graph to answer the questions and write the answers on the lines below.

How many paintings did Olivia paint? _____

How many paintings did Levi paint? _____

How many paintings did Oscar and Mila paint altogether? _____

How many more paintings did Clare paint than Oscar? _____

How many paintings did everybody paint in all? _____

ANSWER KEY

Page 5

Phonics

Initial Sounds
Say the names of the pictures and write the missing letters to complete the words below.

_g_ irl	_f_ rog	_b_ utterfly
_t_ ruck	_c_ lock	_k_ itten
_l_ ion	_r_ ake	_a_ pple

What two words above start with the same sound but different letters?

clock   kitten

Page 6

Phonics

Final Sounds
Say the names of the pictures and write the missing letters to complete the words below.

tige _r_	watermelo _n_
ow _l_	elephan _t_

Draw something in each box that ends with each letter's sound.

n   m   s

Page 7

Phonics

Beginning Consonant Blends
br cr fr gr tr
When you see two consonants together, you blend the sounds. The blended sounds are called consonant blends.
Say the names of the pictures and listen for the consonant blend sounds. Write the missing letters on the lines below.

_f_ _r_ og	_g_ _r_ apes
_b_ _r_ oom	_t_ _r_ umpet
_c_ _r_ ab	_g_ _r_ een

Page 8

Phonics

Beginning Consonant Blends
bl cl fl pl
Read the sentences and use the pictures as clues to help you find the missing consonant blends. Write the missing consonant blends on the lines below. Use the list of the beginning consonant blends above to help you.

The butterfly drinks nectar from a _fl_ ower.

I like to _pl_ ay with my friends.

My brother builds a tower with _bl_ ocks.

My baby sister likes to carry a _bl_ anket.

I can tell time on a _cl_ ock.

I help my mom _cl_ ean the table.

Earth is the _pl_ anet we live on.

Page 9

Phonics

Beginning Consonant Blends
sl sn sk sp
Say the names of the pictures and listen for the consonant blend sounds. Write the missing letters on the lines below.

_s_ _n_ ake	_s_ _t_ airs	_s_ _k_ unk
_s_ _p_ ider	_s_ _p_ oon	_s_ _k_ ip
_s_ _k_ ates	_s_ _n_ owman	_s_ _t_ ar

Page 10

Phonics

Ending Consonant Blends
nt nk mp nd nt
Sometimes consonant blends are at the end of a word. Say the names of the pictures and listen for the consonant blends. Write the missing letters on the lines below.

te _n_ _t_	pi _n_ _k_	pai _n_ _t_
ju _m_ _p_	peppermi _n_ _t_	sta _m_ _p_
la _m_ _p_	sa _n_ _d_	ha _n_ _d_

Page 11

Phonics

Beginning Consonant Digraphs
th sh ch
A digraph is made when two consonants blend together and create one sound.

Examples: think   ship   chick

Say the names of the pictures and write the missing letters to complete the words below.

_s_ _h_ eep	_c_ _h_ urch	_c_ _h_ eese
_t_ _h_ ree	_t_ _h_ umb	_s_ _h_ oe
_c_ _h_ air	_t_ _h_ orn	_s_ _h_ irt

Page 12

Phonics

Beginning Consonant Digraphs
kn wr gn
These consonant digraphs are special because you do not hear the first letter, but you do hear the second letter's original sound (instead of a new sound).

Examples: knee   wrap   gnaw

Say the names of the pictures and write the missing letters to complete the words below. Then color the pictures.

_k_ _n_ ife	_k_ _n_ ot	_w_ _r_ eath
_w_ _r_ ist	_g_ _n_ at	_g_ _n_ ome

Page 13

Phonics

Ending Consonant Digraphs
ch ck th sh
Sometimes consonant digraphs are at the end of words.
Say the names of the pictures and write the missing letters on the lines below.

chi _c_ _k_	fi _s_ _h_	ba _t_ _h_
di _s_ _h_	sandwi _c_ _h_	bea _c_ _h_
du _c_ _k_	tee _t_ _h_	sti _c_ _k_

Read the text below. Then circle the words with a digraph at the beginning, middle, or end.

My family took a trip to the beach. We brought a picnic with yummy sandwiches. We also packed peaches and juice! We went swimming in the ocean and saw a bunch of fish.

223

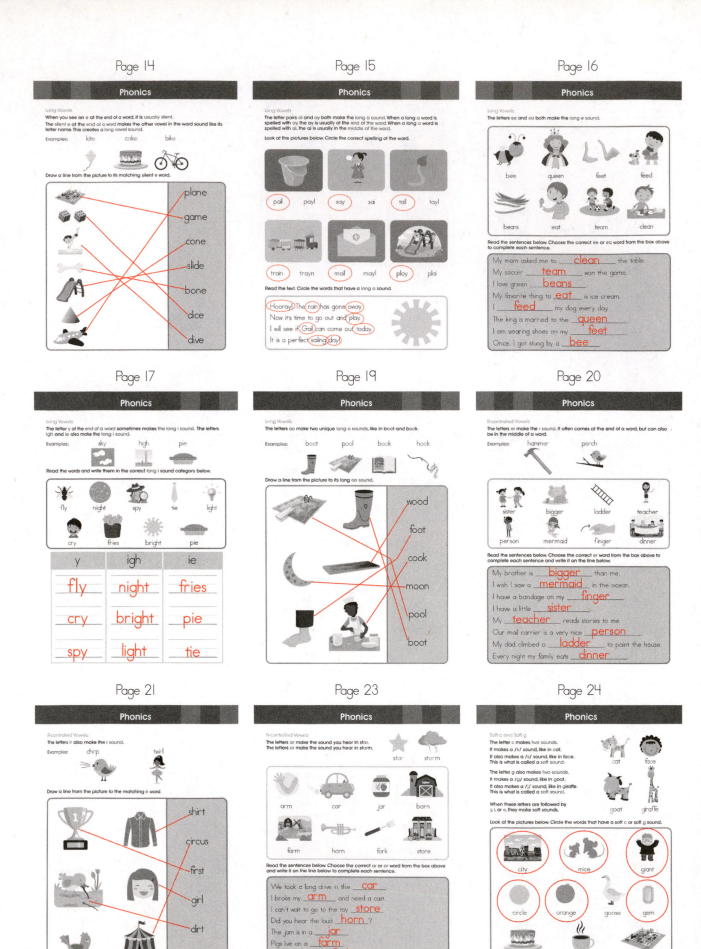

Page 28

Author's Purpose

Author's Purpose
When an author writes, they do so for one or more reasons: to entertain, to inform, or to persuade.

Writing to Entertain
Writing to entertain means the author wrote the text for the pleasure of reading. Books that are written to entertain are usually fiction.

Circle the books below that were written to entertain.

Page 29

Author's Purpose

Writing to Inform
Writing to inform means the author wants to give readers facts or teach them about something. Books that are written to inform are usually nonfiction. They can be books about something or someone, or they can show readers how to make or do something.

Circle the book that was written to inform.

Writing to Persuade
Writing to persuade means the author wants to convince you to believe something or do something based on reasons and evidence. Books that are written to persuade state an opinion about a topic and then provide facts and explain why it is important to believe what the author is saying.

Circle the book that was written to persuade.

Page 31

Reading Comprehension

Summarizing
Summarizing means explaining the details of the story in just a few words. A story summary should answer these questions: who, what, when, where, and why?

Write a few words or a sentence on each line to answer the questions and summarize "Hannah's Soccer Game."

Who is the main character in the story?

Hannah.

What is happening in the story?

Hannah plays soccer and her team plays for the championship.

When is it happening?

During the school year

Where is it happening?

On the soccer field

Why did the author write this story? What is the author's purpose?

To tell a story about Hannah and her team winning the championship. It is a story written to entertain.

Page 32

Reading Comprehension

Main Idea and Important Events
The main idea is what the text is about.

Complete the graphic organizer by writing the main idea and three important events about "Hannah's Soccer Game" in the boxes below.

Main Idea

Hannah's team wins the championship!

Important Event	Important Event	Important Event
Hannah enjoys being a defender.	*Hannah played in every game.*	*Hannah scored the winning goal in the championship game.*

Page 35

Vocabulary

Unknown Words
If there is a word you do not know in a sentence, studying the words around the unknown word and the illustration can help you figure out what the unknown word means.

Read the sentences below and use the words in each sentence to figure out the missing word.

swooping   dizzy   heights

Max doesn't like flying too high up in the sky because he is afraid of _**heights**_.

After Max spun around too quickly, he got _**dizzy**_ and forgot where he was.

Jax is _**swooping**_ down quickly to get some food.

Page 38

Reading Comprehension

Main Idea and Important Details
Complete the graphic organizer below by writing the main idea and three important events about "Max, the Happy Hawk" in the boxes below.

Main Idea

Max gets glasses.

Important Event	Important Event	Important Event
Max gets dizzy when he flies.	*Wise Owl suggests Max needs glasses.*	*Once Max has glasses, he doesn't get dizzy anymore.*

Page 40

Reading Comprehension

Finding Important Details
Readers can find important details to answer questions about something they have read. Important details can be found in sentences and illustrations.

What sentence in the story "Max, the Happy Hawk" told you that Max did not like to look down? Write that sentence from the story on the lines below.

He did not like to look down when he was up high.

Who told Max to go see Wise Owl? Write that sentence from the story on the lines below.

Max's friend, Pax, suggested he talk to Wise Owl.

Circle the picture that shows how Max felt when he got glasses.

Circle the word that describes how Max felt after he got glasses.

happy   scared   sad

Page 42

Fiction and Nonfiction

Fiction and Nonfiction
A fiction story is a story that is not true.
A nonfiction story is a story that is true. It has facts and information.

Read the stories below and decide whether they are fiction or nonfiction stories. Circle your answer below each story.

A Field Full of Carrots
Rita Rabbit loved eating carrots. She loved them so much that she ate them all day long. One day, Rita woke up and there were no carrots in the house. She went outside to her garden, and there were no carrots there either! Rita began to get very hungry. She ran and ran all the way to Farmer Frank's field. She found carrots as far as the eye could see. "Thank goodness!" she said. Farmer Frank let Rita bring home two big baskets of carrots to share with her family.

(Fiction)   Nonfiction

Dinosaurs
Dinosaurs cannot be found on Earth anymore. They are extinct. That means there are no more living dinosaurs. Scientists have researched dinosaurs by digging up fossils and dinosaur bones. They found that some dinosaurs ate meat and some ate plants. There used to be many different kinds of dinosaurs.

Fiction   (Nonfiction)

Page 43

Nonfiction

Table of Contents
The table of contents tells readers which topics can be found in a book and the pages where they can be found.

Use the table of contents above to answer the questions. Write your answers on the lines below.

How many topics are in the book?

Four

Which topic begins on page 4?

Where Horses Live

Which topic begins on page 6?

Horse Babies

If I want to find out what horses eat, what topic will help me learn this information?

What Horses Eat

Nonfiction

Photos and Illustrations

Nonfiction text often has photographs and realistic illustrations. They are meant to give the reader a realistic idea of what things actually look like.

Sometimes the pictures or illustrations have captions that provide more information about the picture or illustration.

Butterflies need to live near a water source, such as a stream or pond.

Use the illustration and caption to answer the questions below.

What do you see in the illustration?

Trees, grass, flowers, rocks, and butterflies

What does the caption tell you about the illustration?

Butterflies need to live near a water source.

Nonfiction

Labels

Labels give more information to the readers.
Nonfiction books use labels to identify details in the pictures.

Use the labeled butterfly diagram to answer the questions. Write your answers on the lines below.

How many legs does a butterfly have?

Six

Are the antenna on the top or bottom of a butterfly's body?

On the top

What is the head attached to on a butterfly's body?

The thorax

Reading Comprehension

Venn Diagrams

A Venn diagram can be used to compare how two or more things are alike and how they are different.

The overlapping parts of a Venn diagram include information about how things are alike. The parts that don't overlap include information about how things are different.

Think about two different kinds of sharks from "Super Shark Facts" and write how they are alike and different in the Venn diagram below.

Great White Sharks
- good sense of smell
- eat seals and small whales
- can swim fast
- been around for millions of years

How are they the same?

- biggest fish in the ocean
- eat krill

Whale Sharks

ABC Order

ABC Order

Putting words into ABC order means they are in the order of the alphabet. Sometimes you need to look at the second or third letter to decide the correct order.

A B C D E F G H I J K L M
N O P Q R S T U V W X Y Z

Put the words below in alphabetical order. You can use the alphabet letters above to help you figure out the correct order for each box.

1. bread
2. bride
3. butterfly
4. island
5. pumpkin

1. candy
2. car
3. cello
4. music
5. zebra

Consonants and Vowels

Consonants and Vowels

Some of the letters of the alphabet are vowels, including a, e, i, o, u, and sometimes y. The rest of the letters in the alphabet are called consonants.

Read the words below and circle the vowels in red and circle the consonants in blue.

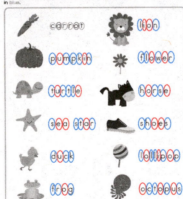

carrot — lion
pumpkin — flower
turtle — horse
sea star — shoes
duck — lollipop
frog — octopus

Consonants and Vowels

Short and Long Vowels

Vowels most commonly make short vowel sounds, as in dad, jet, gift, fog, and bug. Vowels can also make long vowel sounds, as in gate, bean, bike, blow, and music. Look at the pictures and write the missing short or long vowels on the lines below. Say the sounds as you write the letters.

c a t   m u sic
p i g   pl a ne
d o g   p i e
b a ll   sn a ke
d u ck   c u be
t o p   b o wl
h a t   h a y
p o t   b i ke
f a n   wh a le
b a t   n i ght

Consonants and Vowels

Short and Long Vowels

Read the words in the bubbles. Color the short vowel words red and the long vowel words blue.

toe, lips, made, grow, make, sneak, snow, bake, hugs, leg, throw, blow, peak, map

Word Families

Word Families •**There are other correct answers**

Word families are words that all share the same word chunk or letters.

Examples: cat, hat, mat, and flat are all part of the at word family.

Write beginning sounds to create words in each word family below. Try to fill all the lists.

ock	all	ing	ish
s ock	b all	r ing	f ish
r ock	c all	s ing	d ish
m ock	f all	k ing	w ish
l ock	m all	w ing	s w ish
b l ock	s mall	b r ing	v a n ish
c l ock	s t all	t h ing	f i n ish

Word Families

Word Families •**There are other correct answers**

Write beginning sounds to create words in each word family. Try to fill all the lists.

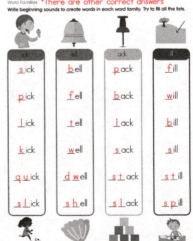

ick	ell	ack	ill
s ick	b ell	p ack	f ill
p ick	f ell	b ack	w ill
l ick	t ell	l ack	b ill
k ick	w ell	s ack	s ill
qu ick	d well	s t ack	s t ill
s l ick	s h ell	s l ack	s p ill

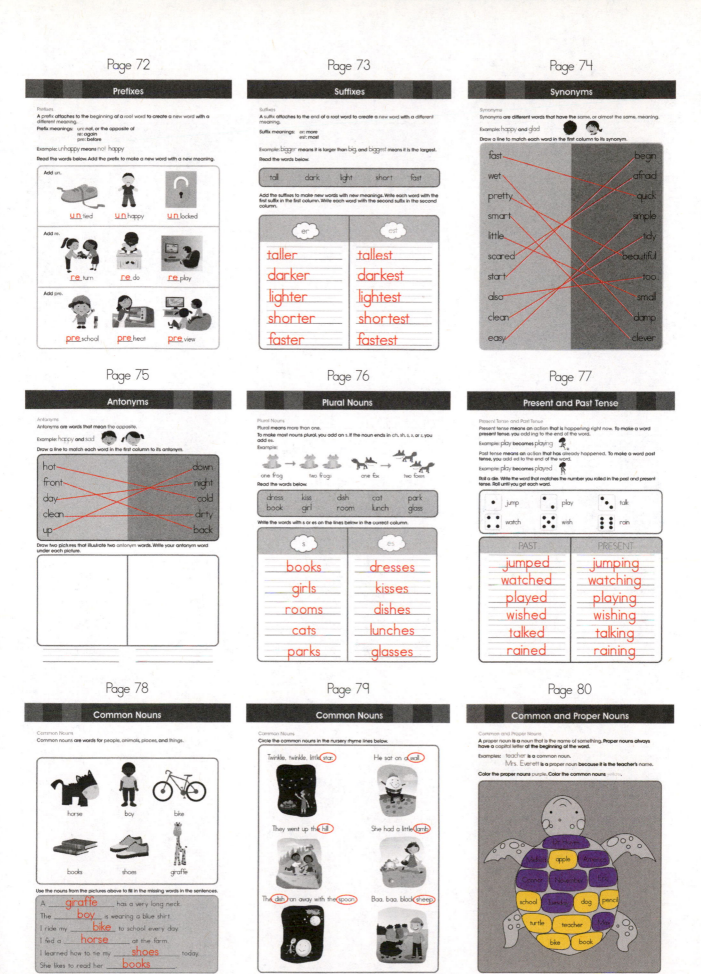

Page 72
Prefixes

Prefixes
A prefix attaches to the beginning of a root word to create a new word with a different meaning.
Prefix meanings: un: not, or the opposite of
re: again
pre: before

Example: unhappy means not happy

Read the words below. Add the prefix to make a new word with a new meaning.

Add un.
un tied   un happy   un locked

Add re.
re turn   re do   re play

Add pre.
pre school   pre heat   pre view

Page 73
Suffixes

Suffixes
A suffix attaches to the end of a root word to create a new word with a different meaning.
Suffix meanings: er: more
est: most

Example: bigger means it is larger than big, and biggest means it is the largest.

Read the words below.

tall   dark   light   short   fast

Add the suffixes to make new words with new meanings. Write each word with the first suffix in the first column. Write each word with the second suffix in the second column.

er	est
taller	tallest
darker	darkest
lighter	lightest
shorter	shortest
faster	fastest

Page 74
Synonyms

Synonyms
Synonyms are different words that have the same, or almost the same, meaning.

Example: happy and glad

Draw a line to match each word in the first column to its synonym.

fast — quick
wet — damp
pretty — beautiful
smart — clever
little — small
scared — afraid
start — begin
also — too
clean — tidy
easy — simple

Page 75
Antonyms

Antonyms
Antonyms are words that mean the opposite.

Example: happy and sad

Draw a line to match each word in the first column to its antonym.

hot — cold
front — back
day — night
clean — dirty
up — down

Draw two pictures that illustrate two antonym words. Write your antonym word under each picture.

Page 76
Plural Nouns

Plural Nouns
Plural means more than one.
To make most nouns plural, you add an s. If the noun ends in ch, sh, s, x, or z, you add es.
Example:
one frog → two frogs   one fox → two foxes

Read the words below.

dress   kiss   dish   cat   park
book   girl   room   lunch   glass

Write the words with s or es on the lines below in the correct column.

s	es
books	dresses
girls	kisses
rooms	dishes
cats	lunches
parks	glasses

Page 77
Present and Past Tense

Present Tense and Past Tense
Present tense means an action that is happening right now. To make a word present tense, you add ing to the end of the word.
Example: play becomes playing

Past tense means an action that has already happened. To make a word past tense, you add ed to the end of the word.
Example: play becomes played

Roll a die. Write the word that matches the number you rolled in the past and present tense. Roll until you get each word.

jump   play   talk
watch   wish   rain

PAST	PRESENT
jumped	jumping
watched	watching
played	playing
wished	wishing
talked	talking
rained	raining

Page 78
Common Nouns

Common Nouns
Common nouns are words for people, animals, places, and things.

horse   boy   bike
books   shoes   giraffe

Use the nouns from the pictures above to fill in the missing words in the sentences.

A giraffe has a very long neck.
The boy is wearing a blue shirt.
I ride my bike to school every day.
I fed a horse at the farm.
I learned how to tie my shoes today.
She likes to read her books.

Page 79
Common Nouns

Common Nouns
Circle the common nouns in the nursery rhyme lines below.

Twinkle, twinkle, little star.

He sat on a wall.

They went up the hill.

She had a little lamb.

The dish ran away with the spoon.

Baa, baa, black sheep.

Page 80
Common and Proper Nouns

Common and Proper Nouns
A proper noun is a noun that is the name of something. Proper nouns always have a capital letter at the beginning of the word.

Examples: teacher is a common noun.
Mrs. Everett is a proper noun because it is the teacher's name.

Color the proper nouns purple. Color the common nouns yellow.

Page 81

Common and Proper Nouns

Common and Proper Nouns

Identify the pictures as common or proper nouns. Then write the word common or proper next to each picture.

bear **common**   squirrel **common**

tent **common**   hat **common**

Mr. Hunter **proper**   Seattle **proper**

United States **proper**   octopus **common**

Zac **proper**   Hannah **proper**

tiger **common**   moose **common**

Kristin **proper**   castle **common**

koala **common**   April **proper**

Page 82

Adjectives

Adjectives

Adjectives are words that describe how things feel, smell, taste, or sound.
Read the words in each row. Circle the two words that describe each picture.

(pink)   hot   (slippery)   dirty

(fluffy)   (gray)   black   smelly

cold   (bright)   purple   (hot)

Add an adjective that describes the noun in each sentence.

Kittens are _____

Candy is _____

Rain is _____

Fire is _____

Friends are _____

Dogs are _____

Alligators are _____

Page 84

Verbs

Verbs

Verbs are words that tell what a noun is doing. They are action words.

Use the picture above to help you complete the sentences. Write the words on the lines below.

The friends are __**throwing**__ snowballs.
The kids are __**running**__ in the snow.
The girl is __**swinging**__ on the swing.
The moms are __**talking**__ to each other.
The dad is __**drinking**__ coffee.
The boy and girl are __**building**__ a snowman.
The people are __**skating**__ on the ice.

Page 85

Verbs

Verbs

Read the words below.
Color the winter hats that have verbs on them.

skip   bird   hand   wiggle   nose

cup   talk   game   run   laugh

Read the sentences below. Then circle the correct verb to complete each sentence.

I love to (jumping (jump)) rope.

I am (play (playing)) a game.

The cow is (eat (eating)) the grass.

Can we (go) going) to the playground?

I love (drink (drinking)) hot chocolate!

Page 87

Verbs and Adverbs

Verbs and Adverbs

Circle the verb and underline the adverb for each sentence below. Then write the verb and adverb for each sentence in the correct columns.

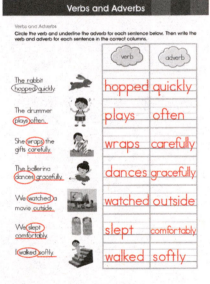

verb	adverb
hopped	quickly
plays	often
wraps	carefully
dances	gracefully
watched	outside
slept	comfortably
walked	softly

The rabbit (hopped) quickly.

The drummer (plays) often.

She (wraps) the gifts carefully.

The ballerina (dances) gracefully.

We (watched) a movie outside.

We (slept) comfortably.

I (walked) softly.

Page 88

Compound Words

Compound Words

Compound words are two words put together to make a new word with a new meaning.

Example: paint and brush = paintbrush

Look at the pictures below and say the words. Put the two words together and write the compound word on the lines below.

+ = **sunflower**

+ = **horseshoe**

+ = **catfish**

+ = **eyeball**

+ = **pigpen**

+ = **doghouse**

+ = **cupcake**

+ = **lipstick**

Page 89

Compound Words

Compound Words

Draw a line to match two socks to make a real compound word. Write your compound words on the lines below.

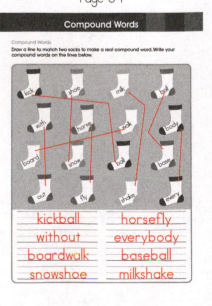

kick   shoe   milk   ball

with   horse   walk   body

board   snow   ball   base

out   fly   shake   every

kickball   **horsefly**

without   **everybody**

boardwalk   **baseball**

snowshoe   **milkshake**

Page 90

Contractions

Contractions

Contractions are two words made into one word. An apostrophe is placed where some of the letters are left out of the new word.

Example: do not = don't

Draw a line from the words to the matching contractions.

did not — isn't
was not — didn't
have not — wasn't
is not — haven't

I will — you'll
you will — I'll
they will — she'll
she will — they'll

I am — she's
he is — I'm
she is — he's
it is — it's

Page 91

Contractions

Contractions

Read the two words in each box and write its contraction on the lines below. Then color the animals.

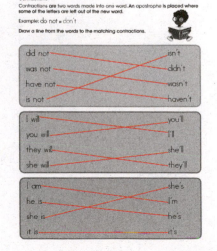

did not **didn't**   was not **wasn't**   have not **haven't**

is not **isn't**   I am **I'm**   he is **he's**

she is **she's**   it is **it's**   I will **I'll**

you will **you'll**   they will **they'll**   she will **she'll**

228

Page 92

Writing Sentences

Sentences

Every sentence starts with a capital letter and ends with a punctuation mark. Statement sentences tell the reader something. They start with a capital letter and end with a period.

Read the statement sentences. Rewrite them on the lines below using a capital letter at the beginning and ending with a period.

i like to play at the park
I like to play at the park.

let's go swimming today
Let's go swimming today.

i live in the United States
I live in the United States.

the frog jumped over the log
The frog jumped over the log.

i can feed the chickens on the farm
I can feed the chickens on the farm.

my name is Emma
My name is Emma.

i can skate really well
I can skate really well.

Page 93

Writing Sentences

Sentences

Question sentences ask the reader a question. They start with a capital letter and end with a question mark.

Read the question sentences. Rewrite them on the lines below using a capital letter at the beginning and ending with a question mark.

what is your favorite sport
What is your favorite sport?

do you know how to tie your shoes
Do you know how to tie your shoes?

can you come out to play today
Can you come out to play today?

what is your favorite color
What is your favorite color?

what grade are you in
What grade are you in?

who is your best friend
Who is your best friend?

where do you live
Where do you live?

Page 94

Writing Sentences

Sentences

Exclamation sentences tell the reader about something that is exciting, scary, or surprising. They start with a capital letter and end with an exclamation mark.

Commands are short sentences with only a noun and verb. Commands also start with a capital letter and end with an exclamation mark.

Read the sentences. Rewrite them on the lines below using a capital letter at the beginning and ending with an exclamation mark.

look at that scary monster
Look at that scary monster!

i won the race
I won the race!

look at the beautiful fireworks
Look at the beautiful fireworks!

sit down
Sit down!

go. team
Go. team!

it is my birthday today
It is my birthday today!

look out
Look out!

Page 107

Number Patterns

Count by Twos

Skip counting can make counting faster!

Skip count the flowers by 2s per flowerpot. Write the increasing numbers on the lines below as you count.

2 4 6 8 10
12 14 16 18 20
22 24 26 28 30
32 34 36 38 40

Page 108

Number Patterns

Count by Fives

Skip counting by 5s is even faster!

You can count the arms of sea stars quickly because each sea star has five. Write the increasing number of arms on each one as you count each sea star by 5s.

5 10 15 20
25 30 35 40
45 50 55 60
65 70 75 80
85 90 95 100

Page 109

Number Patterns

Count by Tens

Skip counting by 10s is even faster!

Skip count the jelly beans in each jar by 10s. Write the numbers on the lines below as you count.

10 20 30
40 50 60
70 80 90
100

Page 110

Place Value

Hundreds, Tens, and Ones

Look at the illustrations and write the hundreds, tens, and ones on the lines below.

Example:

1 hundred and 5 tens and 7 ones = 157

2 hundreds **2** tens **6** ones = **226**   **3** hundreds **5** tens **3** ones = **353**

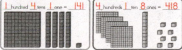

1 hundred **4** tens **1** one = **141**   **4** hundreds **1** ten **8** ones = **418**

1 hundred **7** tens **4** ones = **174**   **3** hundreds **6** tens **5** ones = **365**

Page 111

Place Value

Real Situations

Read the math stories and answer the questions.

Libby, a librarian, loves her library books. She has shelves of 100 library books, boxes of 10 books, and single books.

How many books does Libby have? **464**

Ben, a zookeeper, needs to feed the seals! He has crates of 100 fish, buckets of 10 fish, and some single fish.

How many fish does Ben have to feed the seals? **387**

Page 112

Place Value

Expanded Form

Write the numbers below in expanded form.

Example: 359 = 300 + 50 + 9

671	283
600 + 70 + 1	**200 + 80 + 3**
105	920
100 + 0 + 5	**900 + 20 + 0**
762	334
700 + 60 + 2	**300 + 30 + 4**
547	999
500 + 40 + 7	**900 + 90 + 9**
418	856
400 + 10 + 8	**800 + 50 + 6**

Page 113

Place Value

Comparing Numbers
Use greater than >, less than <, or equal to = to make the equations true and write the number below each expanded number.

$300 + 20 + 1$ ⦵< $300 + 60 + 1$
321   361

$900 + 50 + 3$ ⦵> $900 + 50 + 1$
953   951

$600 + 0 + 0$ ⦵< $600 + 10 + 1$
600   611

$200 + 90 + 9$ ⦵> $200 + 80 + 9$
299   289

$100 + 10 + 1$ ⦵= $100 + 10 + 1$
111   111

$500 + 30 + 7$ ⦵< $500 + 40 + 7$
537   547

Page 114

Place Value

Ordering Numbers
Put the following numbers in order from greatest to least.

352, 125, 501
501 , 352 , 125

623, 603, 671
671 , 623 , 603

901, 989, 931
989 , 931 , 901

232, 721, 43
721 , 232 , 43

Put the following numbers in order from least to greatest.

438, 223, 639
223 , 438 , 639

222, 202, 220
202 , 220 , 222

521, 512, 152
152 , 512 , 521

726, 861, 672
672 , 726 , 861

Page 115

Place Value

Even Numbers
When the digit in the ones place is 0, 2, 4, 6, or 8, the number is an even number. This means the number can be decomposed into two equal groups.

Example:
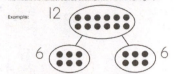

Create equal groups for these numbers. First fill the top oval with the total number of dots. Then divide that number into two equal groups and fill in the bottom two ovals with an equal number of dots.

Page 116

Place Value

Odd Numbers
When the digit in the ones place is 1, 3, 5, 7, or 9, the number is an odd number. This means the number will have one left over when decomposed into two equal groups.

Example:
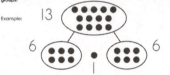

Create equal groups for these numbers. First fill the top oval with the total number of dots. Then divide that number into two equal groups and fill in the bottom two ovals with the correct number of dots. There should be one number left over, so be sure to draw a dot to represent that number between the two ovals.

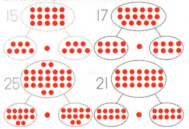

Page 118

Operations

Adding 2-Digit Numbers by Traditional Regrouping
Regrouping means changing ones into tens or tens back into ones. Adding two-digit numbers often requires regrouping.
Look at the example below. If the numbers in the ones column add up to more than 9, we need to regroup.

Example: $45 + 19 = $ ___
First add the ones.
$5 + 9 = 14$.
14 is more than 9. We need to regroup.
14 means 1 ten and 4 ones.
Put the 4 in the ones column and the 1 at the top of the tens column.
Now add the tens. $10 + 40 + 10 = 60$.
Put your tens and ones together: $60 + 4 = 64$.
The sum is 64.

Tens	Ones
1	
4	5
+ 1	9
6	4

Solve the equations by regrouping. Write the sums in the boxes below.

Tens	Ones		Tens	Ones		Tens	Ones		Tens	Ones
1			1			1			1	
2	6		4	5		2	2		4	7
+ 4	7		+ 3	8		+ 3	9		+ 3	6
7	3		8	3		6	1		8	3

Tens	Ones		Tens	Ones		Tens	Ones		Tens	Ones
1						1			1	
7	3		4	6		3	6		2	9
+ 1	8		+ 2	8		+ 5	5		+ 6	8
9	1		7	4		9	1		9	7

Page 119

Operations

Adding 2-Digit Numbers by Traditional Regrouping
Solve the equations by regrouping. Write the sums in the boxes below.

Tens	Ones		Tens	Ones		Tens	Ones		Tens	Ones
1			1			1			1	
4	9		2	6		4	7		7	4
+ 1	8		+ 1	7		+ 3	5		+ 1	7
6	7		4	3		8	2		9	1

Tens	Ones		Tens	Ones		Tens	Ones		Tens	Ones
1			1							
1	9		1	1		2	3		4	4
+ 2	7		+ 2	9		+ 3	7		+ 1	6
4	6		4	0		6	0		6	0

Tens	Ones		Tens	Ones		Tens	Ones		Tens	Ones
1			1			1				
7	9		1	5		5	7		1	6
+ 1	3		+ 2	7		+ 3	7		+ 3	5
9	2		4	2		9	4		5	1

Tens	Ones		Tens	Ones		Tens	Ones		Tens	Ones
1			1			1			1	
1	5		1	7		7	7		3	9
+ 4	6		+ 2	4		+ 1	8		+ 3	5
6	1		4	1		9	5		7	4

Page 120

Operations

Adding 3-Digit Numbers by Traditional Regrouping
When adding three-digit numbers, regrouping is often needed too.
Look at the example below. If the numbers in a place value column add up to more than 9 in the ones column or 99 in the tens column, we need to regroup.

Example: $545 + 269 = $ ___
First add the ones.
$5 + 9 = 14$.
14 is more than 9.
We need to regroup.
14 means 1 ten and 4 ones.
Put the 4 in the ones column and the 1 at the top of the tens column.
Now add the tens. $10 + 40 + 60 = 110$.
110 is more than 99. We need to regroup.
Put a 1 at the bottom of the tens column to represent 10 and a 1 at the top of the hundreds column to represent 100.
Now add the hundreds. $100 + 500 + 200 = 800$.
Put your hundreds, tens, and ones together:
$800 + 10 + 4 = 814$.
The sum is 814.

Hundreds	Tens	Ones
1	1	
5	4	5
+ 2	6	9
8	1	4

Solve the equations by using traditional regrouping. Write the sums in the boxes below.

Hundreds	Tens	Ones		Hundreds	Tens	Ones		Hundreds	Tens	Ones
	1			1	1				1	
7	1	4		2	9	5		3	5	7
+ 2	1	7		+ 1	2	7		+ 2	9	5
9	3	1		4	2	2		6	5	2

Page 121

Operations

Adding 3-Digit Numbers by Traditional Regrouping
Solve the equations by using traditional regrouping. Write the sums in the boxes below.

Hundreds	Tens	Ones		Hundreds	Tens	Ones		Hundreds	Tens	Ones
1	1			1				1		
6	1	5		3	4	7		2	7	9
+ 1	9	5		+ 4	6	9		+ 6	1	9
8	1	0		8	1	6		8	9	8

Hundreds	Tens	Ones		Hundreds	Tens	Ones		Hundreds	Tens	Ones
1	1			1					1	
3	1	3		2	2	6		1	0	5
+ 1	9	7		+ 4	7	4		+ 3	9	9
5	1	0		7	0	0		5	0	4

Hundreds	Tens	Ones		Hundreds	Tens	Ones		Hundreds	Tens	Ones
	1							1		
6	9	5		5	8	3		4	3	7
+ 2	2	6		+ 1	4	9		+ 3	8	9
9	2	1		7	3	2		8	2	6

Hundreds	Tens	Ones		Hundreds	Tens	Ones		Hundreds	Tens	Ones
1	1			1				1		
5	9	4		4	8	4		6	0	5
+ 3	7	8		+ 3	8	7		+ 3	2	7
9	7	2		8	7	1		9	3	2

Page 122

Operations

Adding 3-Digit Numbers by the Column Method
Knowing place value can help you solve addition equations using the column method.

Example:
First add each place value column and keep each sum in the correct column.

Hundreds	Tens	Ones
2	8	3
+ 6	2	9
8	10	12
9	1	2
1		
9	1	2

The 12 in the ones column is 1 ten and 2 ones, so you need to move 1 ten to the tens place.
11 tens means you need to move 1 ten to the hundreds place.

Now the sum is:
$283 + 629 = 912$

Solve the equations using the column method.

Hundreds	Tens	Ones
3	6	7
+ 2	3	8
5	9	15
6	10	5
	0	

$367 + 238 = 605$

Hundreds	Tens	Ones
1	2	6
+ 4	9	5
5	11	11
6	12	1
	2	

$126 + 495 = 621$

Operations

Adding 3-Digit Numbers by the Column Method.
Solve the equations using the column method.

Hundreds	Tens	Ones
4	7	2
+ 1	4	9
5	11	11
6	12	1
	2	

$$472 + 149 = 621$$

Hundreds	Tens	Ones
1	2	8
+ 3	7	5
4	9	13
5	10	3
	0	

$$128 + 375 = 503$$

Hundreds	Tens	Ones
6	7	9
+ 2	4	5
8	11	14
9	12	4
	2	

$$679 + 245 = 924$$

Hundreds	Tens	Ones
1	3	8
+ 6	2	4
7	5	12
	6	2

$$138 + 624 = 762$$

Operations

Subtracting 2-Digit Numbers by Traditional Regrouping

Subtracting tens and ones sometimes requires regrouping.
Look at the example below. If the top number in a place value column is smaller than the bottom number, you need to regroup.

Example: 45 - 18 = ___
First subtract the ones.
5 - 8 = ___
5 is less than 8. We need to regroup.
That means we need to take 1 set of ten
from the tens column and move it to the ones column.
Now subtract the ones. 15 - 8 = 7.
Next subtract the remaining tens. 30 - 10 = 20.
Put your tens and ones together: 20 + 7 = 27.
The difference is 27.

Tens	Ones
3	15
4	5
- 1	8
2	7

Solve the difference equations by regrouping. Write the differences below.

Tens	Ones
4	12
5	2
- 4	6
0	6

Tens	Ones
1	13
2	3
- 1	6
0	7

Tens	Ones
3	17
4	7
- 2	8
1	9

Tens	Ones
2	13
3	3
-	9
1	4

Tens	Ones
2	14
3	4
- 2	6
0	8

Tens	Ones
3	15
4	5
- 2	7
1	8

Tens	Ones
4	16
5	6
- 3	7
1	9

Tens	Ones
5	17
6	7
- 4	8
1	9

Operations

Subtracting 2-Digit Numbers by Traditional Regrouping
Solve the equations by regrouping. Write the differences below.

Tens	Ones
2	15
3	5
- 1	7
1	8

Tens	Ones
3	17
4	7
- 1	8
2	9

Tens	Ones
4	13
5	3
- 1	7
3	6

Tens	Ones
2	10
3	0
- 1	8
1	2

Tens	Ones
4	12
5	2
- 2	8
2	4

Tens	Ones
2	19
3	9
- 1	9
2	0

Tens	Ones
3	16
4	6
- 3	8
0	8

Tens	Ones
4	14
5	4
- 4	7
0	7

Tens	Ones
5	13
6	3
- 4	8
1	5

Tens	Ones
6	12
7	2
- 5	6
1	6

Tens	Ones
7	17
8	7
-	9
6	8

Tens	Ones
8	13
9	3
- 2	9
6	4

Operations

Subtracting 3-Digit Numbers by Traditional Regrouping
Solve the equations by regrouping. Write the differences below.

Hundreds	Tens	Ones
	10	
5	0	10
6	1	0
- 4	4	7
1	6	3

Hundreds	Tens	Ones
6	2	11
7	3	1
- 1	8	6
5	4	5

Hundreds	Tens	Ones
	14	
6	4	14
7	5	4
- 1	6	8
5	8	6

Hundreds	Tens	Ones
	11	
5	1	13
6	2	3
- 2	9	5
3	2	8

Hundreds	Tens	Ones
	12	
6	2	13
7	3	3
- 5	6	7
0	6	6

Hundreds	Tens	Ones
	16	
2	6	13
3	7	3
- 2	9	6
0	7	7

Hundreds	Tens	Ones
	16	
8	6	12
9	7	2
- 3	8	3
5	8	9

Hundreds	Tens	Ones
	12	
5	2	12
6	3	2
- 1	8	5
4	4	7

Hundreds	Tens	Ones
	17	
8	7	12
9	8	2
- 3	9	4
5	8	8

Operations

Subtracting 3-Digit Numbers by Traditional Regrouping
Solve the equations by regrouping. Write the differences below.

Hundreds	Tens	Ones
	12	
7	2	10
8	3	0
- 2	4	6
5	8	4

Hundreds	Tens	Ones
	12	
5	2	11
6	3	1
- 1	5	5
4	7	6

Hundreds	Tens	Ones
	12	
4	2	14
5	3	4
- 1	4	6
3	8	8

Hundreds	Tens	Ones
	12	
4	2	10
5	3	0
- 2	7	1
1	5	9

Hundreds	Tens	Ones
	10	
7	0	15
8	1	5
- 5	6	9
2	4	6

Hundreds	Tens	Ones
	12	
6	2	11
7	3	1
- 1	7	5
5	5	6

Hundreds	Tens	Ones
	15	
6	5	11
7	6	1
- 3	7	8
2	8	3

Hundreds	Tens	Ones
	11	
1	1	13
2	2	3
- 1	7	9
0	5	4

Hundreds	Tens	Ones
	12	
6	2	11
7	3	1
- 2	8	7
3	4	4

Operations

1-Step Word Problems

Sometimes math equations are hidden in word problems. Read each addition or subtraction word problem carefully and write an equation that shows the unknown number. Solve your equation and write the answer on the line.

Example: Ella makes bracelets for her friends and family. She had 89 but gave some away. She has 56 bracelets left. How many did she give away?

$$89 - ? = 56 \qquad 89 - 56 = 33$$

Ella gave away __33__ bracelets.

Oscar collects miniature race cars. He has 29 cars. His friend Caleb has 15 more cars than Oscar. How many cars does Caleb have?

$$29 + 15 = 44$$

Caleb has __44__ cars.

Finn loves the space shuttle. He knows it is 122 feet long and 78 feet wide. How much longer is the space shuttle than it is wide?

$$122 - 78 = 44$$

The shuttle is __44__ feet longer than it is wide.

Operations

1-Step Word Problems
Solve the 1-step word problems. Show your thinking by writing your equations and solving them to find the answers.

Monica sells kayaks. She has sold 27 of them to a group of vacationers. There are still 49 kayaks in her shop. How many kayaks did Monica have when she opened her shop?

$$27 + 49 = 76 \qquad 76$$

Sam is a firefighter. He has 42 firefighter friends working at his station. Then 26 of them move to another fire station. How many firefighters are left at Sam's station?

$$42 - 26 = 16 \qquad 16$$

Jack is setting up 26 tents at his campground. He has already finished setting up 18 tents. How many tents still need to be set up?

$$26 - 18 = 8 \qquad 8$$

Katie has 79 tomato seedlings to plant on her family farm. She has planted 38 seedlings so far. How many tomato seedlings does Katie have left to plant?

$$79 - 38 = 41 \qquad 41$$

Operations

2-Step Word Problems

To solve word problems with two steps, you need to figure out what operations you will need to use for each step. You may need to:

add/add   add/subtract
subtract/subtract   subtract/add

Example: Molly buys 4 shirts and 5 skirts. She returns 2 skirts the next day. How many pieces of clothing did Molly keep?
First step: 4 shirts + 5 skirts = 9 pieces of clothing
Second step: 9 pieces - 2 skirts = 7 pieces of clothing
               Molly kept 7 pieces of clothing.

Solve the 2-step word problems. Show your thinking by writing the equations and solving for each step.

There were 20 people on the bus. Then 4 people got off at the next stop. Later, 8 people got on at the last stop. How many people are on the bus when it arrives at the station?

First step: 20 - 4 = 16   Second step: 16 + 8 = 24

24

Hayley's mom made 26 cupcakes for Hayley's birthday party. Hayley made 10 more. Then Hayley's sister came in and ate 4 cupcakes! Does Hayley have enough cupcakes to serve 30 friends at her party?

First step: 26 + 10 = 36   Second step: 36 - 4 = 32

32

Circle the answer: (Yes, Hayley has enough cupcakes.)
No, Hayley does not have enough cupcakes.

Operations

2-Step Word Problems
Solve the 2-step word problems. Show your thinking by writing the equations and solving for each step.

There are 18 baseballs and 13 volleyballs in the locker room. There are 10 balls used during practice after school. How many balls are left in the locker room?

First step: 18 + 13 = 31   Second step: 31 - 10 = 21

21

The pet store has 46 fish in a large tank and 23 fish in a smaller tank. A lady buys 14 fish in the morning. How many fish does the pet store have now?

First step: 46 + 23 = 69   Second step: 69 - 14 = 55

55

Marcus had 52 markers. He received 12 more as a gift. Then he lost 17 of them at school. Does he have more markers or less markers than he originally had?

First step: 52 + 12 = 64   Second step: 64 - 17 = 47

47

Circle the answer: Marcus has MORE markers.
(Marcus has FEWER markers.)

Page 133

Understanding Multiplication

Rectangular Arrays
A rectangular array is an arrangement of objects in rows and columns in equal groups. Each row has the same number of objects, and each column has the same number of objects.

Example:

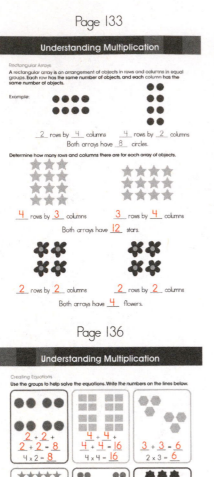

__2__ rows by __4__ columns   __4__ rows by __2__ columns
Both arrays have __8__ circles.

Determine how many rows and columns there are for each array of objects.

__4__ rows by __3__ columns   __3__ rows by __4__ columns
Both arrays have __12__ stars.

__2__ rows by __2__ columns   __2__ rows by __2__ columns
Both arrays have __4__ flowers.

Page 134

Understanding Multiplication

Rectangular Arrays
Determine how many rows and columns there are for each array of objects.

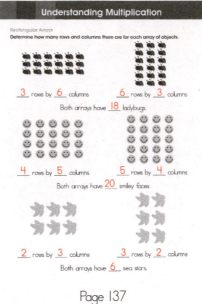

__3__ rows by __6__ columns   __6__ rows by __3__ columns
Both arrays have __18__ ladybugs.

__4__ rows by __5__ columns   __5__ rows by __4__ columns
Both arrays have __20__ smiley faces.

__2__ rows by __3__ columns   __3__ rows by __2__ columns
Both arrays have __6__ sea stars.

Page 135

Understanding Multiplication

Creating Equations
You can find out "how many" by combining the same number, or equal groups, of the same number.

Example: 3 groups of 5 is $5 + 5 + 5 = 15$ or $3 \times 5 = 15$

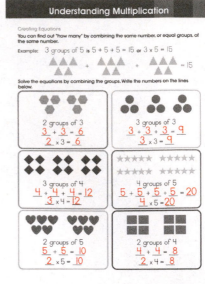

Solve the equations by combining the groups. Write the numbers on the lines below.

2 groups of 3
$3 + 3 = 6$
$2 \times 3 = 6$

3 groups of 3
$3 + 3 + 3 = 9$
$3 \times 3 = 9$

3 groups of 4
$4 + 4 + 4 = 12$
$3 \times 4 = 12$

4 groups of 5
$5 + 5 + 5 + 5 = 20$
$4 \times 5 = 20$

2 groups of 5
$5 + 5 = 10$
$2 \times 5 = 10$

2 groups of 4
$4 + 4 = 8$
$2 \times 4 = 8$

Page 136

Understanding Multiplication

Creating Equations
Use the groups to help solve the equations. Write the numbers on the lines below.

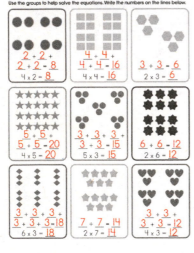

$2 + 2 +$
$2 + 2 = 8$
$4 \times 2 = 8$

$4 + 4 +$
$4 + 4 = 16$
$4 \times 4 = 16$

$3 + 3 = 6$
$2 \times 3 = 6$

$5 + 5 +$
$5 + 5 = 20$
$4 \times 5 = 20$

$3 + 3 + 3 +$
$3 + 3 = 15$
$5 \times 3 = 15$

$6 + 6 = 12$
$2 \times 6 = 12$

$3 + 3 +$
$3 + 3 + 3 = 18$
$6 \times 3 = 18$

$7 + 7 = 14$
$2 \times 7 = 14$

$3 + 3 +$
$3 + 3 = 12$
$4 \times 3 = 12$

Page 137

Regular and Irregular Shapes

Regular and Irregular Shapes
A regular shape has all equal sides and all equal angles. An irregular shape has at least one side that is a different length than its other sides and/or at least one different angle than its other angles.

Example:

regular pentagon   irregular pentagon

Circle the correct type for each shape.

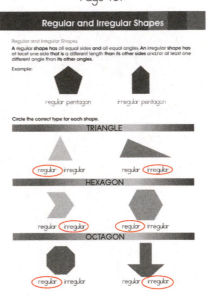

TRIANGLE
(regular) irregular   regular (irregular)

HEXAGON
regular (irregular)   (regular) irregular

OCTAGON
(regular) irregular   regular (irregular)

Page 138

Regular and Irregular Shapes

Regular and Irregular Shapes
Circle the correct type for each shape.

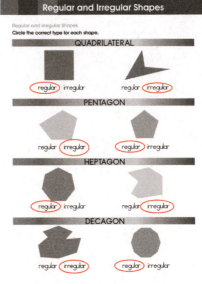

QUADRILATERAL
(regular) irregular   regular (irregular)

PENTAGON
regular (irregular)   (regular) irregular

HEPTAGON
(regular) irregular   regular (irregular)

DECAGON
regular (irregular)   (regular) irregular

Page 139

Shapes and Shares

One Half
One half means a figure is partitioned into 2 equal shares.

Example: one whole   1 out of 2 equal shares or one half

Shade 1 out of 2 equal shares for each shape. Write the missing information below each shape.

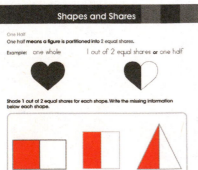

one __half__ of a   one __half__ of a   one __half__ of a
__rectangle__   __square__   __triangle__

one __half__ of a   one __half__ of a   one __half__ of a
__quadrilateral__   __circle__   __quadrilateral__

Page 140

Shapes and Shares

One Third
One third means a figure is partitioned into 3 equal shares.

Example: one whole   1 out of 3 equal shares or one third

Shade 1 out of 3 equal shares for each shape. Write the missing information below each shape.

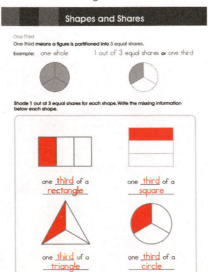

one __third__ of a   one __third__ of a
__rectangle__   __square__

one __third__ of a   one __third__ of a
__triangle__   __circle__

Page 141

Shapes and Shares

One Fourth
One fourth means a figure is partitioned into 4 equal shares.

Example: one whole   1 out of 4 equal shares or one fourth

Shade 1 out of 4 equal shares for each shape. Write the missing information below each shape.

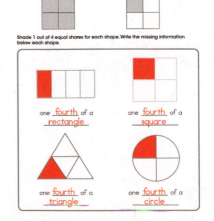

one __fourth__ of a   one __fourth__ of a
__rectangle__   __square__

one __fourth__ of a   one __fourth__ of a
__triangle__   __circle__

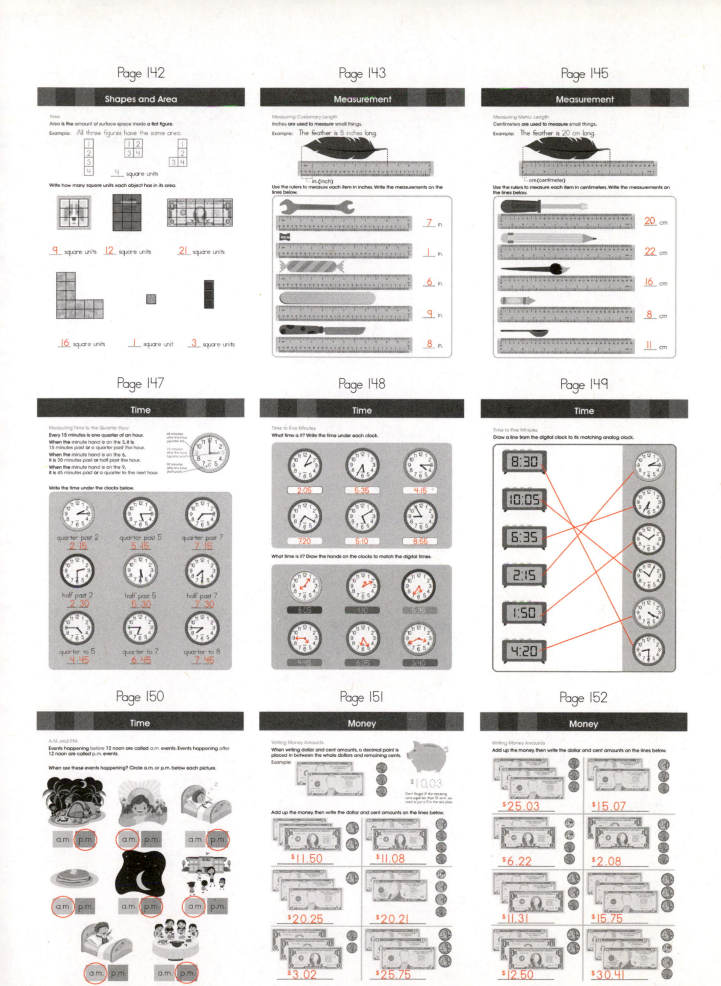

Page 142

Shapes and Area

Area

Area is the amount of surface space inside a flat figure.

Example: All three figures have the same area.

4 square units

Write how many square units each object has in its area.

9 square units   12 square units   21 square units

16 square units   1 square unit   3 square units

Page 143

Measurement

Measuring Customary Length

Inches are used to measure small things.

Example: The feather is 8 inches long.

in. (inch)

Use the rulers to measure each item in inches. Write the measurements on the lines below.

7 in.
1 in.
6 in.
9 in.
8 in.

Page 145

Measurement

Measuring Metric Length

Centimeters are used to measure small things.

Example: The feather is 20 cm long.

cm (centimeter)

Use the rulers to measure each item in centimeters. Write the measurements on the lines below.

20 cm
22 cm
16 cm
8 cm
11 cm

Page 147

Time

Measuring Time to the Quarter Hour

Every 15 minutes is one quarter of an hour.
When the minute hand is on the 3, it is 15 minutes past or a quarter past the hour.
When the minute hand is on the 6, it is 30 minutes past or half past the hour.
When the minute hand is on the 9, it is 45 minutes past or a quarter to the next hour.

Write the time under the clocks below.

quarter past 2   quarter past 5   quarter past 7
2:15   5:15   7:15

half past 2   half past 5   half past 7
2:30   5:30   7:30

quarter to 5   quarter to 7   quarter to 8
4:45   6:45   7:45

Page 148

Time

Time to Five Minutes

What time is it? Write the time under each clock.

2:05   5:35   4:15

7:20   5:10   8:55

What time is it? Draw the hands on the clocks to match the digital times.

8:05   1:10   5:35

4:45   6:25   3:40

Page 149

Time

Time to Five Minutes

Draw a line from the digital clock to its matching analog clock.

8:30
10:05
6:35
2:15
1:50
4:20

Page 150

Time

A.M. and P.M.

Events happening before 12 noon are called a.m. events. Events happening after 12 noon are called p.m. events.

When are these events happening? Circle a.m. or p.m. below each picture.

a.m. (p.m.)   (a.m.) p.m.   a.m. (p.m.)

(a.m.) p.m.   a.m. (p.m.)   (a.m.) p.m.

(a.m.) p.m.   a.m. (p.m.)

Page 151

Money

Writing Money Amounts

When writing dollar and cent amounts, a decimal point is placed in between the whole dollars and remaining cents.

Example:

$10.03

Don't forget if the remaining cents equal less than 10 cents, you need to put a 0 in the tens place.

Add up the money, then write the dollar and cent amounts on the lines below.

$11.50 $11.08

$20.25 $20.21

$3.02 $25.75

Page 152

Money

Writing Money Amounts

Add up the money, then write the dollar and cent amounts on the lines below.

$25.03 $15.07

$6.22 $2.08

$11.31 $15.75

$12.50 $30.41

Money

Writing Money Amounts

Subtract the money with an X on it, then write the equations and totals on the lines below.

Example:

$20.60 - $5.10 = **$15.50**

$35.41 - $10.10 = **$25.31** $4.07 - $2.03 = **$2.04**

$40.60 - $15.25 = **$25.35** $40.30 - $10.10 = **$30.20**

Money

Solving Money Word Problems

Read the word problems and then write an equation to help you find the missing amounts.

Example: Susie had some money in her piggy bank from last week. Today, she earned $5.50 for her weekly chores. Now she has $10.25 in her bank. How much did she have in her bank last week?

? + $5.50 = $10.25
$10.25 - $5.50 = $4.75

Susie had $4.75 in her piggy bank last week.

Jim walks into a store. He has $10.00 to spend. He buys a blue shirt. When he leaves the store, he has $5.25 left. How much did his shirt cost?

$10.00 - ? = $5.25   **$4.75**
$10.00 - $5.25 = $4.75

Candice earned $8.35 for singing at a party. She earned $7.55 for singing at another party. How much money does she have now?

$8.35 + $7.55 = $15.90
$15.90

Terri went to the same store as Jim. She had $15.25 to spend. How much more money does she have to spend than Jim did when he first went into the store? $15.25 - $10.00 = $5.25
$5.25

Data Management

Reading a Picture Graph

A picture graph uses pictures to represent units. The key tells you the unit quantity.

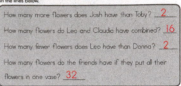

Flowers for Friends   Key: = 1 Flower

Josh	
Toby	
Leo	
Donna	
Claudia	

Use the picture graph to answer the questions about the data. Write your answers on the lines below.

How many more flowers does Josh have than Toby?   **2**

How many flowers do Leo and Claudia have combined?   **16**

How many fewer flowers does Leo have than Donna?   **2**

How many flowers do the friends have if they put all their flowers in one vase?   **32**

Data Management

Reading a Line Plot

A line plot represents the frequency of amounts in a group.

Example: Egg Hunt

The line plot tells you that no students out of 15 found 5 eggs. Three students found 6 eggs. One student found zero eggs.

Answer the questions using the line plot. Write your answers on the lines below. Mr. Smith's gym class was asked to do push-ups without resting. Here are the results:

Push-Up Contest

How many students were able to do 5 push-ups?   **1**
How many students could do one push-up?   **3**
What numbers of push-ups did no students do?   **7 8 10**
What numbers of push-ups were done by three students?   **1 2**

Data Management

Creating a Line Plot

Transfer the collected tally chart data to the line plot below using Xs.

Students with Pets

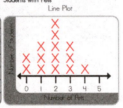

Tally Chart	
Pets	Students
0	II
1	III
2	HHT
3	III
4	I
5	

Answer the questions below. Write your answers on the lines.

How many students own less than 2 pets?   **5**

How many students own more than 2 pets?   **4**

How many pets are owned by three students?   **1   3**

ABC Order

Put the words below in alphabetical order.

1. **antelope**   1. **cat**

2. **apple**   2. **hockey**

3. **butter**   3. **hose**

4. **rooster**   4. **television**

5. **tennis**   5. **violin**

Blends and Sounds

Read the sentences below and use the pictures to help you fill in the missing letters in the words to show the consonant blends.

I can use a **gl**obe.

My favorite color is **bl**ue.

I love my cozy **bl**anket.

I found a four-leaf **cl**over.

Look at the **cl**ouds in the sky.

Blends and Sounds

Say the names of the pictures and fill in the missing letters in the words to show the beginning consonant blends.

green   **gr**ade

drink   **cr**ayon

pretzel   **pr**ice

Blends and Sounds

Say the names of the pictures and fill in the missing letters in the words to show the ending consonant blends.

sta**mp**   wi**nk**

a**nt**   ha**nd**

sta**mp**   pai**nt**

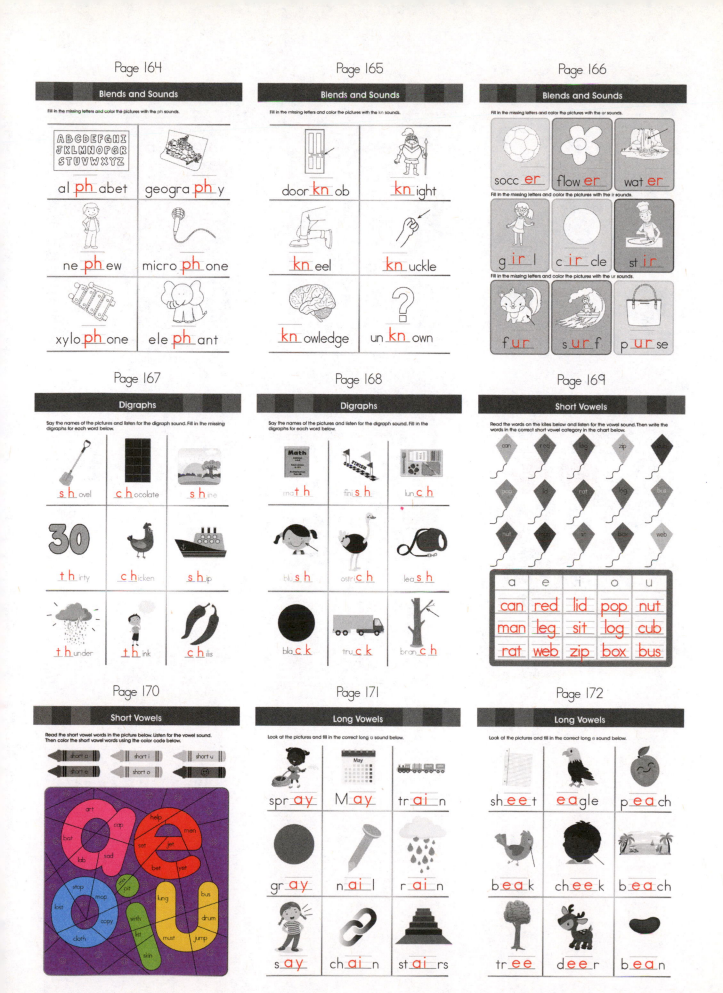

Page 164

Blends and Sounds

Fill in the missing letters and color the pictures with the ph sounds.

al **ph** abet   geogra **ph** y

ne **ph** ew   micro **ph** one

xylo **ph** one   ele **ph** ant

Page 165

Blends and Sounds

Fill in the missing letters and color the pictures with the kn sounds.

door **kn** ob   **kn** ight

kn eel   **kn** uckle

kn owledge   un **kn** own

Page 166

Blends and Sounds

Fill in the missing letters and color the pictures with the er sounds.

socc **er**   flow **er**   wat **er**

Fill in the missing letters and color the pictures with the ir sounds.

g **ir** l   c **ir** cle   st **ir**

Fill in the missing letters and color the pictures with the ur sounds.

f **ur**   s **ur** f   p **ur** se

Page 167

Digraphs

Say the names of the pictures and listen for the digraph sound. Fill in the missing digraphs for each word below.

s **h** ovel   **ch** ocolate   s **h** ine

t **h** irty   **c h** icken   s **h** ip

t **h** under   t **h** ink   **c h** ilis

Page 168

Digraphs

Say the names of the pictures and listen for the digraph sound. Fill in the digraphs for each word below.

ma **t h**   fini **s h**   lun **c h**

blu **s h**   ostri **c h**   lea **s h**

bla **c k**   tru **c k**   bran **c h**

Page 169

Short Vowels

Read the words on the kites below and listen for the vowel sound. Then write the words in the correct short vowel category in the chart below.

can   red   log   zip   bus

pop   lid   rat   leg   bat

nut   man   sit   box   web

a	e	i	o	u
can	red	lid	pop	nut
man	leg	sit	log	cub
rat	web	zip	box	bus

Page 170

Short Vowels

Read the short vowel words in the picture below. Listen for the vowel sound. Then color the short vowel words using the color code below.

short a   short i   short u
short e   short o

art, cap, help, men, bat, cat, jet, lab, sad, bet, yet, stop, mix, pit, bus, mop, lost, copy, with, drum, cloth, list, must, jump, skin

Page 171

Long Vowels

Look at the pictures and fill in the correct long a sound below.

spr **ay**   M **ay**   tr **ai** n

gr **ay**   n **ai** l   r **ai** n

s **ay**   ch **ai** n   st **ai** rs

Page 172

Long Vowels

Look at the pictures and fill in the correct long e sound below.

sh **ee** t   **ea** gle   p **ea** ch

b **ea** k   ch **ee** k   b **ea** ch

tr **ee**   d **ee** r   b **ea** n

Page 173

Long Vowels

Look at the pictures and fill in the correct long i sound below.

l**igh**t   b**i**ke   qu**ie**t

fl**igh**t   cr**y**   d**i**ce

n**igh**t   r**igh**t   s**igh**t

Page 174

Long Vowels

Look at the pictures and fill in the correct long o sound below.

b**oa**rd   r**ow**   b**ow**l

t**oa**d   thr**ow**   l**oa**f

r**oa**r   **oa**tmeal   g**o**

Page 175

Long Vowels

Read the long vowel words in the picture below. Listen for the vowel sound. Then color the long vowel words using the color code below.

long a   long i   long u
long e   long o

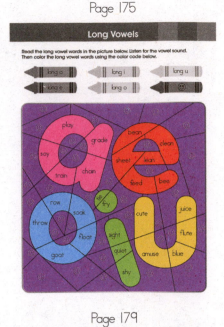

Page 176

Short and Long Vowels

Short and Long Vowels
Read the words in the bubbles. Color the short vowel words red and the long vowel words blue.

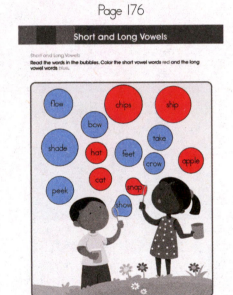

Page 178

Nouns

Read the rhymes below and circle the common nouns.

Meg Yorke eats an (egg) with a (fork).

Big Matt hits the (ball) with a (bat).

Hayley the (clown) is wearing a (crown).

My (dog), Applejack, stole my (snack).

My (friend) Skye baked me a (pie).

A (girl) named Cass drinks out of a (glass).

Page 179

Nouns

Read the rhymes below and circle the proper nouns.

My friend (Lamar) likes to play guitar.

(Uncle Lars) drives very fast cars.

(Jake) likes to make his favorite cupcake.

(Doctor Ray) gave me a shot, and it left a little dot.

My best friend (Shawn) fed the swan.

My family went to the pool with (Mr. O'Doul).

Page 181

Adjectives

Read the sentences below and circle the adjectives in each sentence.

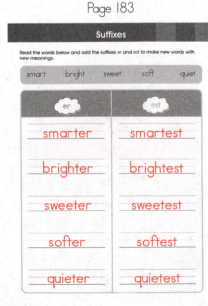

The (brown) dog jumped over the (big) fence.

The marshmallows are (soft) and (chewy).

I got a (new) (summer) skirt.

It is (hot) and (dry) outside today.

I love my (cuddly) (blue) teddy bear.

Look at the (shiny) (gold) crown!

Page 182

Synonyms and Antonyms

Read each sentence below and circle the synonym of the highlighted word.

The towel is wet.	(damp)	dry	hot
The dog is fast.	short	clean	(quick)
The flower is pretty.	hard	(beautiful)	strong

Read each sentence below and circle the antonym of the highlighted word.

The truck is loud.	slow	red	(quiet)
The boy is short.	smart	(tall)	sad
The snail is slow.	dry	(fast)	clean

Page 183

Suffixes

Read the words below and add the suffixes er and est to make new words with new meanings.

smart   bright   sweet   soft   quiet

er	est
smarter	smartest
brighter	brightest
sweeter	sweetest
softer	softest
quieter	quietest

Page 184

Compound Words

Look at the mittens below. Each has a word on it. Match the mittens with words that go together to make a compound word. Write the compound words below and draw a picture for each one to match their new meanings.

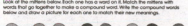

raincoat   backpack

crosswalk   firework

Page 185

Nonfiction

Look at the illustration below and read the labels.

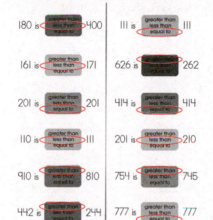

Use the labels to help you answer the questions below.

How many dorsal fins does a shark have?

One

What is on the side of the shark?

Gills

What other things did you learn from the labels?

_____
_____
_____

Page 186

Nonfiction

[farm illustration]

Farms are full of many different types of animals. Each animal is unique. Cows can provide milk and sheep can provide wool.

Use the illustration and caption above to help you answer the questions below.

Describe what you see in the illustration.

A farm with dogs, sheep, cows, a horse, and a duck

What does the caption tell you about the illustration?

Farms have many types of animals and they can help provide for the farm.

Page 200

Comparing Numbers

Look at the numbers below and put the correct symbol in the middle of the two numbers to show if the number is greater than >, less than <, or equal to = the second number.

333 (>) 331   642 (>) 634

734 (<) 754   889 (<) 898

702 (>) 632   433 (>) 343

471 (>) 451   907 (=) 907

Page 201

Comparing Numbers

Look at the numbers below and circle the correct comparison phrase in the middle of the two numbers.

180 is (less than) 400   111 is (equal to) 111

161 is (less than) 171   626 is (greater than) 262

201 is (equal to) 201   414 is (equal to) 414

110 is (less than) 111   201 is (less than) 210

910 is (greater than) 810   754 is (greater than) 745

442 is (greater than) 244   777 is (equal to) 777

Page 202

Place Value

Put the following numbers in order from greatest to least.

488, 484, 844

844 , 488 , 484

337, 733, 373

733 , 373 , 337

594, 194, 694

694 , 594 , 194

222, 111, 101

222 , 111 , 101

776, 777, 779

779 , 777 , 776

123, 321, 213

321 , 213 , 123

Page 203

Place Value

Put the following numbers in order from least to greatest.

352, 125, 501

125 , 352 , 501

623, 603, 671

603 , 623 , 671

901, 989, 931

901 , 931 , 989

438, 223, 639

223 , 438 , 639

222, 202, 220

202 , 220 , 222

521, 512, 152

152 , 512 , 521

Page 204

Place Value

Read the math stories and answer the questions.

Farmer John loves his farm animals. He has barns with 100 animals, pens with 10 animals, and a few animals who wander the farm.

How many animals does Farmer John have? 694

Peggy bakes pies. She has trucks filled with 100 pies, boxes filled with 10 pies, and some pies leftover.

How many pies does Peggy have? 265

Page 205

Place Value

Read the math stories and answer the questions.

Sammy loves to write letters. He has boxes filled with 100 stamps, piles of 10 stamps, and a few stamps left over.

How many stamps does Sammy have? 346

Luke loves his blocks. He has bins filled with 100 blocks, baskets with 10 blocks, and some other blocks on the floor.

How many blocks does Luke have? 449

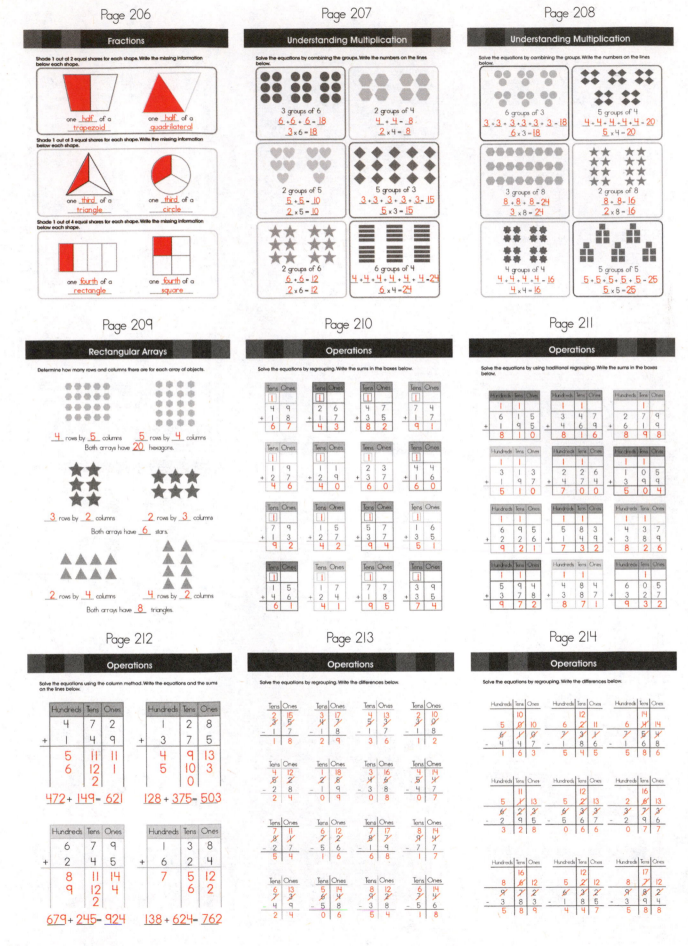

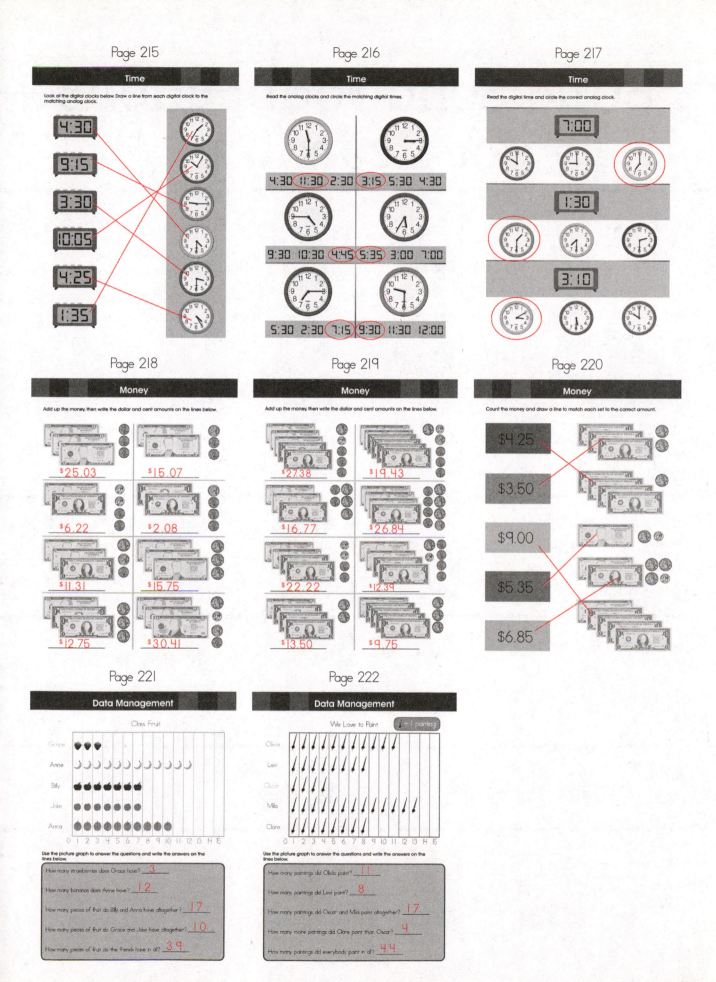

Page 215

Time

Look at the digital clocks below. Draw a line from each digital clock to the matching analog clock.

4:30
9:15
3:30
10:05
4:25
1:35

Page 216

Time

Read the analog clocks and circle the matching digital times.

4:30 (11:30) 2:30 (3:15) 5:30 4:30

9:30 10:30 (4:45) (5:35) 3:00 7:00

5:30 2:30 (7:15) (9:30) 11:30 12:00

Page 217

Time

Read the digital time and circle the correct analog clock.

7:00

1:30

3:10

Page 218

Money

Add up the money, then write the dollar and cent amounts on the lines below.

$25.03 $15.07
$6.22 $2.08
$11.31 $15.75
$12.75 $30.41

Page 219

Money

Add up the money, then write the dollar and cent amounts on the lines below.

$27.38 $19.43
$16.77 $26.84
$22.22 $12.39
$13.50 $9.75

Page 220

Money

Count the money and draw a line to match each set to the correct amount.

$4.25
$3.50
$9.00
$5.35
$6.85

Page 221

Data Management

Class Fruit

Grace
Anne
Billy
Jake
Anna

0 1 2 3 4 5 6 7 8 9 10 11 12 13 14 15

Use the picture graph to answer the questions and write the answers on the lines below.

How many strawberries does Grace have? 3

How many bananas does Anne have? 12

How many pieces of fruit do Billy and Anna have altogether? 17

How many pieces of fruit do Grace and Jake have altogether? 10

How many pieces of fruit do the friends have in all? 39

Page 222

Data Management

We Love to Paint   ✏ = 1 painting

Olivia
Levi
Oscar
Mila
Clare

0 1 2 3 4 5 6 7 8 9 10 11 12 13 14 15

Use the picture graph to answer the questions and write the answers on the lines below.

How many paintings did Olivia paint? 11

How many paintings did Levi paint? 8

How many paintings did Oscar and Mila paint altogether? 17

How many more paintings did Clare paint than Oscar? 4

How many paintings did everybody paint in all? 44

Build Solid Foundations for Learning

Workbooks

Collections

Workpads

Flash Cards

Write & Wipes